DISPATCHES FROM THE DOORYARD

GOT WARRANTS?

TIMOTHY COTTON

Down East Books

Down East Books

An imprint of Globe Pequot

Trade division of The Rowman & Littlefield Publishing Group, Inc.

4501 Forbes Blvd., Ste. 200

Lanham, MD 20706

www.rowman.com

Distributed by NATIONAL BOOK NETWORK

ISBN 978-1-68475-110-5 (paperback)

ISBN 978-1-60893-769-1 (e-book)

♾™ The paper used in this publication meets the minimum requirements of American National Standard for Information Sciences—Permanence of Paper for Printed Library Materials, ANSI/NISO Z39.48-1992.

Contents

GOT WARRANTS?

Introduction

When we decided to produce an entire book focused on episodes of "Got Warrants," I wasn't completely on board with the idea.

I was standing with Michael—my editor—on a cool and overcast autumn morning. We were drinking tepid McDonald's coffee that I had picked up in Belfast, Maine, on the way to his house so we could discuss the idea of where we were headed next. At our last meeting, probably over some other tepid coffee, we talked about writing another book like *The Detective in the Dooryard*.

It had already been determined that I was going to write a total of three more books for Down East Books and, while I was not feeling smug, I was comfortable—actually surprised— with the success that we had seen with my first publication. I fully knew that a book number two could be a very tough sell. While I am not a pessimist, I have heard far too many stories from other writers who crashed and burned when they launched their sophomore writing project.

In my heart, I wanted to produce a fiction book that had been bouncing around inside my surprisingly spacious melon for about five years. I had already done some work on the story line, the characters, and the settings.

Michael was more guarded about that project. His inclination was that a book of "Got Warrants" would be embraced by those who have followed the Bangor Police Department Facebook page for over six years. He likened it to the final chapter of the mildly popular, comedically inclined satirical look at police beat columns that formerly graced the newsprint of small-town newspapers all over America. It could pay homage to the hijinks of hometown lawbreakers who made us shake our heads—and sometimes giggle—while we sipped the second cup of Saturday morning coffee.

While the semi-weekly series had been our most popular feature, I was harboring the notion that I might no longer be a cop by the time the book came out in the late summer or fall of 2021. I was hoping to transition into longer essays about the simple things, Maine life, and get some work done on a darkly humorous book about a grouchy ex-police officer who not only gets off the grid, but works exceedingly hard to never be involved in the sport of enforcing any law—for any reason—ever again. That's how I felt inside. I knew that I could scribble those emotions and notions onto parchment that might later be bound into a novel that very well could become a series of novels. He just sipped and stared as windblown maple leaves dropped around us like poorly trained paratroopers.

"Let's do another book made up entirely of new, never before printed, 'Got Warrants' episodes." I agreed quickly. I trusted his instincts, and I do love to peruse police reports to find a slightly twisted way to relay the information to a reader who might like to laugh about the situations but not at the people.

I've not run photos of suspects on the Bangor Police Department Facebook page for a very long time. I watched the comment sections turn into a sewer of sour remarks when I would provide a photograph of a person we were looking for. I came to the conclusion that if I did a good job in my description of the person, and the crime, then we would find a person of interest just as easily as if I had run their photo on a full-size billboard beside the three Penobscot River bridges that lead in and out of our city.

I wrote this book based on real police reports about real situations that our officers run into every single day. Some of the most bizarre cases were left out because much of what we work through each day is disturbing and too much of it can cause one to sleep very poorly. I've experienced it; so have most all cops. Minor specific details were changed in each piece in order to keep private the identities of those involved.

I wanted to produce a book of "Got Warrants" that would be most comfortable in the rooms where we read the most. Where that room is—in your home—is completely up to you. We made it a bit more compact so a person might keep it in the car to read a few pieces while you wait for a friend or loved one who is in a store looking for some a bit more refined to read.

This is also a book that can be safely left around the house without a worry that the kids will find new vocabulary words that are less than acceptable in most social situations.

By the time you read this, there is a chance that I am no longer employed in the field of law enforcement, so it will be the last "Got Warrants" collection ever produced by Tim Cotton. This makes the book no more valuable, but I hope that you find some humor and hope in what we did with these stories. We are not expecting you to laugh out loud, but we are hopeful that you find yourself smirking or snickering, because that's what I do when I write them. I'd consider it a compliment if you catch yourself doing the same.

Keep your hands to yourself, leave other people's things alone, and be kind to one another. All we have is each other.

—Tim Cotton

1980s Trans Am

While the world might see our job as glamorous, you should know that any officer with a modicum of experience will not shiver with delight when being sent to speak to a person in a blue tank top and blonde ponytail. In high school, there would have been a rush to find someone fitting that description. As a police officer, not so much.

Since most of us have had the pleasure of riding the express train to reality, we know full well that things are never what they seem or even what we hope it will be.

The conductor on that train wears a yellow leisure suit and keeps his floral-patterned nylon shirt buttoned up as far as his xiphoid process. How else would we see his Avon arrowhead necklace?

We know full well that the person we are being sent to investigate will more than likely be drunk and possibly be out looking for his former dream ride—a 1980 Trans Am; the one with the turbo 301-cubic-inch engine and automatic transmission. That's right; like a blue tank top on an intoxicated man, the 1980 Trans Am was never a cool choice.

Once Pontiac removed the manual transmission and the 6.6-liter cast-iron block of American freedom from the T/A, it suddenly became clear that Burt Reynolds was wearing a hair piece, and Sally Field didn't even want to take his hat off.

For the rest of us? We thanked the good lord for the power of the Avon arrowhead necklace and a Zayre's bag full of Brut cologne.

The suspect in question had been yelling at the store clerk as she told him that the bathroom was out of service. The water had been turned off. This was upsetting to him. He then began to yell at other patrons. This makes people uncomfortable. We are used to uncomfortable situations and relish an opportunity to make it better.

When the man threw his beer and donuts on the counter—no, I did not make that part up—in an attempt to make a purchase, she told him that he could buy the donuts but she would not sell him any more intoxicants. This went over like the passing of gas in a house of worship.

While it was evident that the man was a Homer Simpson fan, he still left without the donuts.

The officers located the man and gave him a criminal trespass warning and informed him that he could not return to the store for a period of one year. He said he was sorry for acting out and apologized. Our officers did not make any fashion suggestions for future outings.

A Car Drives into a Bar

A Bangor police officer was assisting another similarly employed cop in dealing with a couple of suspicious persons when he heard a loud bang and tinkling glass from across the street.

Much to his dismay, he observed a small black sedan backing away from a concrete post that had just been struck.

The display of poor driving skills continued as the car backed into a telephone pole some distance away from the original point of impact. The driver then pulled forward and stopped. Obvious damage had been done to both ends of the sedan. Necessary parts of the car had been left near each solidly ensconced waypoint in the driver's brief but devastating attempts at damage-free parking.

Interested in what he had just seen, the officer walked across the street and knocked on the window of the automobile. It was then that he met a young lady who opened the car door, placed her car keys into his hand, and said, "I'm done."

He willingly accepted her resignation.

Her sense of despair was overpowered by the odor of

intoxicants that emitted from within the—now more compact—high-end Asian import.

When he inquired about whether or not the woman had used alcoholic beverages as a pre-ride lubricant, she denied it. However, she did say that she had smoked three bowls of marijuana a couple of hours before the crash(es). Her feeling, verbalized in the most slurred manner imaginable, was that she was no longer affected by the cannabis that she had smoked—with vigor—earlier.

Breath mints, and a well-hung wild cherry air freshener, could not disguise the clear and distinct odor of spirits. He asked her to get out of the automobile and assist him by submitting to a couple of SFSTs (Standardized Field Sobriety Tests). She said, "No."

She explained that her right to drive within the State of Maine had been suspended for the foreseeable future due to previous run-ins with the laws that make it illegal to drink and drive. She was also forbidden to possess or use alcohol, that's why she smoked marijuana as a substance to eliminate her stress.

Still, the nose of a cop rarely lies, and neither did her extremely bloodshot eyes and lack of reasonable depth perception when trying to park a fairly small car.

Her test scores were impressive, and using common core math, then carrying the zero, we discovered that she had shattered her previous test results by tripling our state's mandated minimum standards for being considered too drunk to drive.

Ain't No Party
Like a Clifton Party

It was kind of like a party—a group of six individuals, out of control. They were all fighting in the Airport Mall parking lot. Lots of asphalt, zero chairs or party favors.

We get to attend many strange and inappropriate festivities. We are often invited, but only after things get out of control.

For once, we would like to be there at the beginning—before interpersonal relationships break down because of the excessive use of intoxicants and the calling of horrible names.

Someday, we would like to be there for the finger-foods and discussions about current events, and the fact that Krakatoa is due to erupt in the next few years. But, *noooo*. That doesn't happen.

Officers of the Bangor Police Department arrived and told several of the individuals to calm down or go to jail for the crime of disorderly conduct. This worked long enough for them to gather information that indicated that this little bash had started earlier, in the town of Clifton, Maine. Someone had stolen a firearm, and the Penobscot County Sheriff's Office was already investigating that portion of pre-party preparation.

This preparation should have included an "H." At least it felt that way to our officers.

One man admitted to calling a woman a name that should never be used by a man. The man told officers that he did say it and also is currently dating that same girl's twin sister. Of course, the man had already been head-butted by the young lady prior to our arrival at the now-defunct "Airport Mall Finishing School and Emporium of Proper Language and Manners."

I forgot to mention that someone had grabbed a logging chain just prior to the cops' arrival, and, while it had been put away quickly, it did cause some concerns but no injuries. In the end, the only reason anyone was angry was because of the name that the man had used to upset the young lady. This is not a crime, but it darn sure is dumb.

Thanksgiving dinner this year should be a real treat.

We respectfully request that any further gun-burgling, name-calling, twin-sister-dating, head-butting, chain-swinging extravaganzas remain in the town that originally hosted the event. We have nothing against Clifton as it is a pleasant town—beautiful and quaint, a tasty slice of Americana. However, if Maury Povich reaches out to us, we know where we will be forwarding the phone call.

All parties were advised how to stay away from one another as well as the proper steps to get a protection order.

Attempting to Locate the Amorous

Our officer went to an east-side street in order to investigate loud noises. The complainant revealed to the cop that he could hear noises, and voices, that sounded exactly like two people who could be engaged in the age-old art of interpersonal-relationship building.

He left the complainant's home and stood silently in the street while attempting to pinpoint exactly where he was supposed to deliver the warning for the non-visible couple. After all, his goal was to quiet things down a bit.

He listened intently but could not hear any of what had been reported.

There is a certain relief for an officer who cannot pinpoint the location of obvious, highly vocalized impudicity. The night air gives clarity of thought to a silent blue-clad man who is sent on a mission that he does not want to accept.

He determined if he was called to return to locate the cuddling culprits, he would merely advise them to shut the windows or, from that point on, play their music much louder.

Cops are much more adept at asking folks to turn down Barry White than they are at trying to stop the private (or in this case semi-private) natural progression of life in these United States.

Back in the New York Groove

A man from New York City (we only know because he told us so many times) walked out of a downtown drinkery while screaming several expletive-filled sentences that mentioned shooting—and killing.

While it didn't appear that he was directing the violent speech toward anyone—specifically—he was advised by one of our officers that he needed to keep it down and stop swearing. The man re-entered the business, and that's when the owner told him that they'd had just about enough of him. Did I mention that he told us that he was from New York?

The man said that he wasn't leaving and that he wasn't afraid of jail. Subsequently, he was placed in handcuffs and taken to jail.

He was charged with criminal trespass and disorderly conduct. Oddly, our laws are similar to the laws of New York, but he said that he had never been arrested for this type of behavior before.

The officer shrugged his shoulders and decided not to explain the simplicity of merely moving along as opposed to the second option that had been offered—and accepted.

We are hopeful that—as Ace Frehley did in the 1978 Billboard charted classic—the gentleman can get "back in the New York groove" in the very near future.

Bad Motor Scooter

A man whose pants were making a special appearance—below his knees—was reported to have been seen entering a cellphone repair shop out near the Bangor Mall.

We don't know if he was having trouble getting enough bars for a good signal on his device, but it was clear that he might have visited at least one or two bars before his arrival near our center for commerce and fast-food facilities.

The pride in his stride was compromised—possibly—by the lowered location of his waistband (somewhere near his knees), but he was making it work. We applaud folks who make a commitment and hang in—or hang out—there.

We had dealt with a female acquaintance of the pants-less man earlier that very day.

A witness to an impromptu side show had reported that the lady had fallen off the back of the same man's motorcycle as they set out for a morning ride from their home. It was a lovely day, and she was found to be uninjured. He had already left the residence—without her—when we arrived to investigate. She decided to sit out this ride, and we were pleased with her logical decision.

"Two falls off a scooter does not a genius make."—Yoda (Honest, he did say it).

Back to the man—sans pants—who was last seen seeking a remedy for the signal on his Samsung.

As the cop attempted to enter the cellphone repair center, a bystander pointed out that the man in question had also removed his shirt. She pointed out a plaid and wrinkled short-sleeved 50/50 cotton-blend that was hanging in a nearby row of bushes. We felt positive that the man without pants, or a shirt, would be easy to find walking among other appropriately dressed citizens.

The man was still in the store, and he did stand out from others. The officer asked some pertinent questions. The man claimed he had just been awakened from a nap, and that his wife was across the street completing some business in another establishment. He then blurted out that he was not driving because his license was suspended for some earlier mistakes.

The man said he had not taken any narcotics, either. The officer asked where his shirt was. The man complained that it had been taken by another man. The officer then retrieved the shirt from the bushes and provided it to the gentleman. He put it on. By this time, he had already pulled up his pants. The gesture was appreciated. He then recalled that he might have driven to the location on his motorcycle, but it was also possible that he had driven his car. He just wasn't sure.

Another officer discovered his motorcycle in a parking space just around the corner from the man's current location.

By now, fully dressed, he failed to successfully complete the SFSTs (Standardized Field Sobriety Tests) that were offered to gain clarity about his claimed sobriety. He was taken to jail for operating a motor vehicle under the influence of drugs or alcohol. He was not charged with indecent conduct due to the fact that he was not riding "commando-style" on that particular day.

Bass, but Not the Fish

Right around the beginning of the time we will—in the future—refer to as the pandemic, we received a call from a concerned citizen. That citizen was frustrated. Frustrated because her neighbor was playing music endlessly. His bass was relentless, and I am not talking about a fish.

As a connoisseur of the blessing—and the buzz—that bass bestows upon our recordings of "Bad to the Bone," "Brick House," and "The Ballroom Blitz," color me bad when I say that this made me blue. Bass is the gift that is invitational, omnidirectional, and somewhat perennial.

How could a sound so right turn out to be so wrong? Well, I'll tell you, right after I apologize to the Bee Gees for stealing their thunder, or, if I remember the song correctly, their perfectly blended tenor and soprano vocals.

This bass had no beginning and no end. For the complainant, it was omnipresent, onerous, and endless. This is to say that the man who was the occupant of the apartment where the bass was being generated was unresponsive to her plea for it to stop.

She knocked, and he did not answer. She tried to be the kind of neighbor that we would all love to have. Trying to notify a neighbor of a problem is sometimes—depending on the neighbor—a better method than calling out the po-po.

If the man had been playing "Chevy Van" by Sammy Johns, the bass would have been acceptable. Maybe even some Neil Sedaka, but this music was even more horrific than a continuous loop of "Calendar Girl." Yes, it was bad. And I liked "Laughter in the Rain." Don't judge!

Since the reports are not clear about the selection of the music, we will assume that it was some kind of Country. That is not to say that Country isn't cool. I am merely pointing out that if I ever hear "Country Girl Shake It for Me" again, someone is getting a summons for disturbing my peace.

Our cop showed up, and he knocked. He knocked, and he knocked. He couldn't seem to overcome the ever-present drone of bass, or even the drone that he could see lying on the couch in a perfectly suitable napping posture.

Pandemics tend to make the populace a bit drowsy. I mean, how many episodes of *How It's Made* can a man handle?

Finally, the officer shined the light of justice through the glass and directly into the eyes of the man who would not rise to the occasion. The Maglite (LED version) produces a stupefying flash of white light that even interstellar traveling aliens have complained about when we inadvertently shone them toward the heavens—usually when we slip and fall on the ice.

The man got up and lumbered to the door. He claimed that the music—and accompanying bass—was not too loud. The officer used an age-old trick on the bass-wielding tenant. We call it logic, but some might refer to it as sarcasm. Sometimes the two go together like ebony and ivory.

The cop told the man that he might consider the fact that he had not been able to hear all the knocking that had been going on around him. Knocking from the neighbor, knocking from the cop. Knocking on the window, knocking on the ceiling, twice on the pipes. You get the idea; it was apparent the man was not going to show.

My thanks to Tony Orlando, and Dawn. They sang it better.

The judicious application of logic and kind sarcasm would have made Spock proud. It was as if the gong that is played rhythmically during the intro to "Hells Bells" had been placed directly beside the man's ear pans. He smelled what our cop was cooking, and he suddenly said, "I guess it was pretty loud. I'll turn it down."

You expected a rumble? Nope. It was over in the same way it all started. Two people could now have a nap. Three, if you're counting the cop. Oh, come on, you went there in your head.

The quiet of a cool spring evening was only broken by the crunchy footsteps of a cop who was able to walk away leaving only happy people in his wake. A cop who knows that while a squeaky wheel needs grease, sometimes it's better to utilize a little light when seeking a bit of peace and quiet.

We can't always hear each other when the bass is too loud.

Slow it down today. Just try to listen for the music that plays inside all our heads; you could learn a lot from a song.

I mean, other than "Country Girl Shake It for Me."

Be Like Bob

In December of last year, one of our officers was sent to break up a physical fight between two family members. They were both men, and words had become heated during a discussion about this or that.

I cannot say that alcohol was involved, but there are times when you make assumptions. Assumptions are acceptable. I mean, while the humans of the world love to spout-off that assumptions make an ass out of u and me, the truth of the matter is that reaching that conclusion requires the speaker to have made an assumption.

Our cop pulled his cruiser into the dooryard because the caller was reporting that the men had taken it up a notch by stepping outside to "take care of the business at hand."

Our officer, to remain nameless, pulled up, approached the scene, and began to address the men in the manner that they needed to be addressed.

Now, you've seen cops wear leather search gloves, but those gloves are also be used when you place someone under arrest. You wouldn't believe me if I told you about the myriad substances that people have on their skin. Certainly, there are concerns about body fluids, and in a pandemic, these can be scary.

Humans are a walking petri dish, but sometimes they also can be covered in whatever substance was handy to their opponent during a donnybrook that starts in a kitchen. It seems that mealtime—often at a table—is where people come together and disagreements begin.

I cannot tell you how much mayonnaise, ketchup, and mustard I've had to fight through in order to put the habeus grabus on an offender. Outdoor cookouts are events that seem to mix strong drink with strong opinions. You can imagine the outcome; you've been to a family cookout.

This was not one of those days, but our cop was carrying his personal protective gear—in the form of leather gloves—in a thigh pocket of his uniform pants.

You are probably expecting a story about condiments and a never-ending fistfight, but you are wrong. See, you made an assumption. I am not upset.

I want to tell you about a golden retriever named Bob. Bob is not the dog's actual name. I think that the privacy of golden retrievers also needs to be protected. You assume they aren't mad or upset when we identify them, but you don't really know.

Bob, who was probably sick of the bickering between his housemates, observed that our officer's gloves were sticking out of his pocket. Bob is a retriever. It is apparent that Bob is a good one.

Bob ran up to the officer in order to receive his SVAS (Standard Visitor Applied Scritches)—it's a thing. Cops like dogs, and dogs—like Bob—are always a treat to run into during serious social situations.

The two men had stopped physically whacking each other as they watched Bob work his magic with the new kid on the block.

Bob then noticed the black leather gloves in our cop's pocket. The rest should have been captured by video. Bob did what dogs do and retrieved the gloves and changed the tenor of the entire event. Bob ran away from the officer with the gloves in his mouth. Bob then stopped a short distance away in order to give peace a chance. Well, he taunted the officer hoping that a chase would ensue.

By now the combatants were no longer combatting, and the cop was no longer copping. The peacemaker was now the center of attention. Bob had the gloves and he was not prepared to return them.

Seeing that the fight had stopped, and Bob had his gloves, the cop was able to focus his attention on the dog. Bob was not prepared to give up the gloves.

Each time our officer approached, the golden purveyor of peace would make that move that dogs tend to make. The fake-out. Big brown eyes would look left while furry paws pushed off to go right. You get the idea because it's happened to you. It probably has not happened to you when you were sent to break up a fight between two family members, and you can imagine our cop's embarrassment as he tried to retrieve his personal protective gear from a retriever.

One of the former fighters—because that show had been preempted by Bob—realized the dilemma of the cop, and he went into the house to grab Bob a treat.

Bob was bribed, and being naturally benevolent and bullish on biscuits, he bequeathed the bargaining chips back to the boys without so much as a bark. Bob had done our job.

A peaceful conversation ensued while Bob watched and chewed.

Disagreements were discussed, and our officer walked away without needing the gloves at all. Sure, they were wet with Bob's saliva, but they would dry out.

Be like Bob.

Billiards

We received a call from a facility where they feature billiards as a way for patrons to pass the time between short sips from long-necked bottles.

Apparently, a man had made derogatory comments about the appearance of another man's lady-friend. Our officer found the man and the woman who apparently were at the center of the controversy, as the woman was crying hysterically, and the man was waiting to speak to the officer.

The police officer learned that the lady had been called a name that should, and would, make any one of us upset. The man, standing up for the honor of his girlfriend, asked the purveyor of such slander to apologize for what he had said to his girl.

The man asked the cretin to apologize to the lady and all would be forgiven. He said, and witnesses back up the fact, that he told the man that he did not want any trouble, but he did feel like the man should say he was sorry for upsetting the lady.

At that point, the cretin swung at Buford (not his real

name), and Buford began to bounce the dullard's head off the pool table located conveniently to his left.

It should be noted that we would rather have been called before the violence ensued, but it did appear that the man was only physically defending himself from attack after asking for a simple and kind apology.

Sometimes it is better to apologize.

Buford (not his real name) was then attacked from his right by the brother of Dullard #1. From this point on, I will refer to the second brother as Dullard #2 in order to keep the story straight.

Dullard #2 fared no better than Dullard #1 when attacking Buford. He found himself being bounced off the same pool table with ease as Buford attempted to convey to them his disappointment through the application of Newton's First Law.

Both of the Dullards slipped away quickly after their subsequent pounding, and neither of them apologized to the nice young lady.

The officer asked Buford (not his real name) if he would be interested in having us charge the Dullards, if they were found within a reasonable amount of time.

Buford said it would not be necessary as he does not typically utilize the services of law enforcement. He said he did appreciate our attention to the matter when called upon to respond.

This leads me to a closing poem:

Calling her fat, there's no need of that,
for your mother did raise you correctly.
Warnings were needed, but not one was heeded,
so you bounced off the table abjectly.
We thought you were dumb, but then here he comes,
flailing his fists so cold and unfriendly.
As billiard games go, you moved far too slow,
and your quick loss was enjoyed by many, immensely.
Apologize quicker, you'll seem all the slicker
when you act nice, and be kind, intensely.

Blazer Blasphemy

The clerks at a local doughnut shop reported that an "older male with many missing teeth and wearing a tan blazer" was being vulgar to all the patrons.

While this might be every man's dream job in retirement, it was not well-received by the folks who wanted a coffee with two creams, hold the vulgarity. Throwing on a blazer in your retirement years adds a flair to an otherwise dull day of swearing at those who are taking a moment to fry your doughnuts.

I am a big fan of the blazer as an accoutrement. I like plaid, but a solid navy blue makes a statement. And it adds a perfect background palette for the powdered sugar to present itself to those who might otherwise be unable to determine if you have had your daily dose of doughnuts. Nothing says "devil-may-care" like the freckling of powdered sugar on a dark blue cloak sewn by J.C. Penney's finest tailors. Throw in a spot of strawberry jelly on the tip of a properly folded pocket square, and you have yourself a downright dapper display of all that is good in decorative doughnut daywear.

One of our officers found the man and gave him a notice

to stay out of the lobby. The man called the officer many names, which is something he is used to. The nattily dressed character refused to sign the trespass notice. He did agree to leave, however, and that's really all we were shooting for. He moved on. The blazer did add an air of class to his tirade. "Dress for the job you want, not the job you have," is always good advice.

Blazin' Up a Fatty

Blazin' up a fatty while scrubbing your dirties might seem like a superb and supreme way to pass the time until the Tide Pods do the job for which they were intended; we get it.

On a nice day at the laundromat, you might even want to step outside, hop in the driver's seat of your Sentra, and select one of many fine radio stations serving the greater-Bangor region—bad idea. People call us about those things, and we then have to stop by. No one really wants to see us; we know this.

A bunch of quarters, a Tide pod, an iPod, and fresh bud can equal a relaxed outlook on the day and a basket of clean grundies. The issue is that "smoking the weed" is not an approved public activity.

Now, before you get all "you're killin' me with your rules and stomping my buzz," I understand. One of the specific rules of our new-found freedom is that marijuana is not supposed to be smoked in public, or in the driver's seat.

Getting behind the wheel with a stick of fiery delightfulness is not approved. Please just follow the rules, and we will just wave on our way by to the pastry shop. Maybe we will see you there.

The man in his car enjoying the sunbeam was very understanding and did not realize it was a bad idea. He had to go throw his stuff in the dryer, so we didn't stay long. No, he was not summoned, just warned.

Rules—ruining everything since the beginning of time.

Bunion Kisser

An officer was called to a local big-box store to take a report of suspicious activity. The complainant—a woman—said that she was approached by a man who asked her if he could kiss her feet.

I know from years of spending time in a polygraph room that many people can be strange. Even people you think you know and assume are very normal tend to do strange things.

Heck, you do strange things, but we hope you don't do this.

The woman was in aisle 20 when the man approached and relayed to her that he had a strange request. She thought he might ask her to grab some cereal from the top shelf, possibly request directions to the soup aisle—but, no—he wanted to kiss her feet. He practically begged her.

She did just what she should do, she said, "No." But this man was no quitter.

As he continued to plead with her to kiss her feet, she finally acquiesced.

I would never suggest this as the way to get a perverted

little knave to stop asking, but I think she felt that it would make him go away. She said he could kiss just her shoe.

You know what's gonna happen now, don't you?

Yes, the little pervert dropped down on all fours and did exactly as he pleased. He kissed the skin just above the top of her shoe.

I want to clarify that most of us refer to this area as the ankle, possibly the instep.

Yes, yes, I know, ladies; you all would have drop-kicked the man directly in the teeth. This lady did not.

She was incensed by the whole thing, got a good description, and went immediately to the restroom to wash and sanitize her foot; to this, we say, good call. She also called us.

The pestering perverted pedi-phile—a five-foot-five-inch camo-clad foot-fetish freak—had wandered off toward the front of the store.

I want to write funny things about this event, but even I cannot do that. I share it because we never suggest giving in to a pervert.

Even if they make a promise to do something that seems innocuous, they cannot be trusted to follow simple requests.

Walk away, notify store officials, call us on your cellphone. You can also wave down almost any man because most of us would be glad to be involved in ejecting any overzealous bunion kisser before he osculates all over your Manolo Blahniks.

Seriously, just say, "No."

For the record, we have attempted to gain video footage (yeah, you knew that was coming) of the event, but security cameras did not capture video in that area of the store.

The man was wearing a camo jacket; this is not helpful for identification in Maine during hunting season—or the other eleven months of the year.

These times do try us.

Can I Wash that For You?

A man who was raising funds to buy back his parrot from a local pawn shop was arrested for the crime of disorderly conduct.

The charges did not stem from the pawning of the parrot, but because he was washing automobiles on State Street using water that he was carrying—in pails—up from the bank of Kenduskeag Stream.

When the stream hits low tide, much of the water in the shallow pools has a rusty yet muddy hue. The glacier-dropped granite sedimentation suspended in the waters that were lovingly hand-dipped from the stream can really burnish the clear coat that protects the typical modern-day automotive finish.

Maine river gravel can be very abrasive. Even more abrasive than the unrequested cleansing was the man's gruff personality. He demanded that they pay him—in cash—for, essentially, destroying the paint jobs on their automobiles

Frankly, his sponge appears to have been utilized for cleaning out the empty cage of his—now-pawned—parrot.

When the man became enraged with law enforcement officials for shutting down his street-side handwashing business, he took his shopping cart full of supplies and threw them down the stairway that led to the scenic walkway near the stream.

He was arrested and taken to the county jail. We received no word on the whereabouts of the parrot. We are hopeful the accrued daily interest charged by the pawnbroker does not wash away the man's ongoing interest in his beloved bird.

Canadian Shoplifter

A man who stole spray cheese, white cheddar Cheez-Its, and whiskey was confronted at a local supermarket by their professional loss-prevention officers. Our officer arrived just before the thief began taking hits from the already opened can of Cheez Whiz.

We've all done it, don't be so haughty and claim you have never been involved in the delivery of copious amounts of liquid cheese through the age-old squirting delivery system. The difference, or, what separates us from this man, is the fact that we—hopefully—had already paid for it.

While our officer did summons the individual to court for the attempted theft, he would still like to apologize for assuming that the man was a Canadian. Shortly after the presentation of the summons, the man said he was actually from Bangor.

We have relegated our police officer to the police department library to review our policy on profiling shoplifters by guessing their nation of origin based only on the items they have hidden down their pants.

We have asked him to write, "I will not assume people who drink cheap whiskey and Cheez-Its are from Canada" at least two hundred times.

In the officer's defense, he has watched every episode of *The Trailer Park Boys* and *Letterkenny*. His dream was to have a destination wedding at a Rush concert. However, he later settled on serving warm whiskey and Kraft Dinner at the reception, right after reciting vows in front of a minister who did a very poor impression of a seminary-trained Nova Scotian man of the cloth.

I pronounce you man and wife, eh?

Canadian (Whisky) Thanksgiving

The caller told our dispatcher that he phoned in to report that he had just observed a man lying on the ground under the Penobscot Bridge. The caller was concerned for the man's well-being. Our officer was sent to investigate.

Upon the cop's arrival, he found the man in the position normally described as down and out for the count. The officer gently nudged the man back to consciousness. The man in the sauce-induced stupor finally opened one eye and whispered, "Give me a minute."

Many of our cops have been called kind and considerate. This particular officer had been raised by Canadians. He waited for a few moments, but, as the man fell back asleep the POIQ (Peace Officer In Question) gently nudged him again. The man yelled out, "Hooh-Hah!"

Comfortable with the fact that the man was alive and well, the officer then surveyed the area for liquor, not because he is Canadian (although that could be one factor) but because he felt strongly that the man's condition was probably caused by whisky (spelled without the "e," because that's what a good Canadian would do). It was then he saw the bottle of Fireball.

The man yelled out "Hooah" about five to seven more times and then offered the cop a sip from his bottle. The policeman declined.

The man then invited the uniformed purveyor of justice to a Thanksgiving celebration that was to be held under the bridge around five o'clock that very afternoon. The cop had already celebrated Canadian Thanksgiving back in October, and he was well aware that the American holiday wouldn't take place for a few more weeks. But he played along and said he would not be able to make it.

The man suddenly sat up and noticed the idling black-and-white police interceptor parked nearby. He looked up at the officer and said, "Where'd they come from?" It was then, and only then, that the man realized that the kind Canadian, who nudged him ever so gently, was a police officer.

The inebriated celebrant stood up, grabbed his Fireball whisky, fist bumped the cop, and thanked him for checking on him. He wandered off down the riverbank.

Oh, that Fireball. Such a festive concoction of just the right amount of whisky with a touch of cinnamon.

Of course, in the spirit of the holiday season, I penned a quick poem about the under-bridge encounter of the drunken kind:

Holidays come early
when the drinkers become surly
and Canadian cops wake them up with a nudge.

The cop might have let you nap
if the whisky had been capped,
he probably wouldn't have made you budge.

You most likely saved some money,
poutine is never funny—
fried potatoes covered with sludge!

Be thankful the officer was merry;
it could've gotten scary
and ended with cold turkey and a judge.

Cautious Inebriation

The driver of the car pulled up to the yellow blinking light and came to a full stop. Since an amber signal only urges caution to a driver, the maneuver—or lack of any maneuvering at all—begged the attention of a police officer assigned to watch for this kind of thing when watching for drunk drivers.

Our young officers are astute observers. Astute observing is something learned from hours on an Xbox, or long periods gripping the controller of a PlayStation 3 or 4. While their parents believed they were learning nothing, we have found that these new kids blink far fewer times per minute than the rest of us.

A car waiting at a blinking yellow will sometimes cause the followers to unsheathe their middle digits rather quickly. Sometimes it is followed by the overzealous application of the horn button and loudly delivered coarse language. Since the car and driver were alone in the intersection, none of this occurred.

The car finally started moving forward. The cop followed. At the next stop sign, the driver never touched the brakes, and drove right through the intersection. Could this be a George Costanza–inspired driver working on her own rendition of the famous episode about opposite day?

The cop hit blue lights and siren—sometimes referred to as the noise and the blueberries—and stopped the car on a straight stretch of road leading to the town line. The officer approached the driver and immediately detected the slight scent of the nectar of bad decisions, the Devil's Kool-Aid, loudmouth soup, or, in this case, liquid license remover.

The driver said that she had not been drinking and that she was new to the area. Soon after, she told the cop that she was heading to the store for cigarettes, was trying to find gas, and that she needed pet food.

These are all reasonable answers to the questions that he didn't ask her, but with so many choices delivered in such a staccato manner, he felt strongly that she was making it all up.

We are not saying that this list of locations and reasons could not occur in conjunction with one another, but she also did poorly on her field sobriety tests.

When the cop asked her to rate herself on a scale from zero-to-ten for drunkenness and clarified that zero was considered stone-cold sober and ten was severely inebriated, she offered that she was a five. This can be considered halfway-to-hammered and she was arrested. Once she took her intoxilyzer test it was confirmed that her assessment was true, and she was taken to jail.

Clean Up After Yourself

A cop was sent to the doughnut shop to kick out some unruly patrons. When he arrived on the scene, he was able to ignore the sweet and sultry call of lonely pastries beckoning him from their individualized cooling racks on the other side of the glass divider. He tried to focus on the job at hand.

There were a few folks who had sugar-and-crumbed their way out of the good graces of the late-night hostess, who was probably working two jobs to make ends meet.

They had spilled soda, coffee, crumbs, and sadness all over the floor. One of the men in the group advised the pleasant lady of all that is raised and glazed that they were not going to leave. She needed help.

The cop told them all to get out, and they immediately complied with his wishes. They did not withhold a few poorly delivered doughnut jokes, but from their appearance, they knew them all; I am not talking about the jokes.

As they began to exit, the officer called two of the more able-bodied patrons back to the table. He offered them the lonely industrial-sized broom, and, its closet-mate, the mop.

The officer told them that since they made the mess, they should—in turn—clean it up.

They did.

We are not saying they did a great job, but it gave the lone clerk a small amount of satisfaction as she watched them wield the broom and mop handles with—sloppy—aplomb.

She had visions of the four-foot-long, smoothly worn ash handles being utilized for human popsicle sticks. Those thoughts were reserved for only one of the men in the group who had given her a very hard time. She tried to wash those thoughts right out of her mind, as she was raised right.

Thoughts, like those, should be reserved for the drive-thru customers who demand that she read back to them every doughnut that she has in stock. Typically, those same folks ask for the only doughnut that she didn't mention. She digressed.

Once the area was spotless, the officer took the mop and broom and returned them to the closet. The group left, but not without giving him the one-fingered salute we are so ac-customed to seeing.

Yes, he probably had a doughnut. We cannot begrudge him the opportunity to consume the world's most perfect food with a lady who wanted a little reasonable conversation. He was careful not to get any crumbs on the floor.

Crack Pipe Storage

A lady who was arrested on an outstanding warrant on Ohio Street was asked if she was holding anything prohibited before they took her into the jail for processing.

She said that she had been storing a crack pipe—for a friend—and did not want to take it into the jail and later find herself charged for something that clearly doesn't belong to her.

The officer asked her to tell him where it was. She said it was down the back of her pants. He asked her how long it had been since she had seen her friend, and she said it had been a few days, and the pipe had been stored—there—since that time.

The cop who asked the questions did a quick mental checklist. It included some consideration about all the long-term storage possibilities and pitfalls.

In the end, the prisoner willingly retrieved it without any fanfare. I will only say that the pipe was placed into a plastic bag and put into the evidence locker. You know, in case her friend came looking for it while this lady was in jail.

The owner still hasn't come to claim her pipe. We aren't holding our breath.

Creatures Carrying
Tiny Trampolines

A Bangor officer was sent over to Hancock Street to investigate why "multiple people wearing animal onesies" were walking down the street.

This is strange enough; however, the officer was given additional information from the caller that indicated the folks in the animal costumes were carrying small trampolines.

Knowing the officer quite well, I guarantee he said a little prayer on the way to the call. It probably went something like this: "Please, please, please, be there when I arrive. Please, please, please. Amen."

The fuzzy-clad creatures (with tiny trampolines) were nowhere to be found when the officer arrived at the scene of the sighting.

He was sad.

Admit it, you are, too.

Dale Carnegie Discourse

A fully clothed man was making substantial monetary contributions to a program designed to cause other people to take off their own clothing.

My financial advisor has reiterated to me that programs like this have no monetary upside, unless my goal is to start investing in other long-term housing prospects, as it could cause me to be ejected from my current place.

Yes, the man was at a strip club.

Due to the man's voracious appetite for intoxicants, he had become a bit of a handful for those who run the facility in our "garmentless" district. Our cops met with the individual in order to facilitate the management's desire to provide an empty chair for other investors who wanted to waste resources during the fool-hardy viewing of semi-clothed humans.

The man had ignored the bouncer's advice to leave the premises. Officers utilized language learned in the non-mandatory, but well-advised, attendance to the Dale Carnegie course.

Winning friends and influencing people by yelling "Get out" should really be taught during week number one.

The man did not appear to be moved by the phraseology. Instead, he began to spew curse words that would upset anyone's mom. Adding the term, "We will be taking you to jail if you do not leave" caused the stationary to become mobilized as if by some unseen force.

While the now-mobile miscreant had discovered enough sobriety to ask some stupid questions, he did exit the facility.

He attempted to walk straight but was unable to do it well. His voice trailed off as he moved slowly into the cold night.

Since our men of justice did not want to yell across the lot, patrons who were standing nearby watching the spectacle overheard one of officers saying, "The crooked paths of men cannot be straightened through the use of strong drink."

Dearly Departed

One of our officers was dispatched to attend to a situation in which a woman was reportedly "thrashing around" in the next apartment.

Thrashing around sometimes leads to excessive noise. Excessive noise was really the gist of the complaint; the description of "thrashing around" was just the description from the complainant. Always keep in mind that the caller might be reporting only their perception of events that are unfolding, and then we show up to clarify what the activity might be.

We went because that's what we do.

When the officer arrived, he found three men leaving the apartment at a rapid pace. He inquired what all the fuss was about. One of the men said that a female inside the apartment was "freaking out." Freaking out is just the one person's perception of activity. The cop now had two things to investigate. One of those issues was "thrashing around," and one was "freaking out."

You might be concerned if you were the cop. Neither one

of the aforementioned activities are illegal. The noise that might come from freaking out or thrashing around could possibly rise to the level of disorderly conduct. That is illegal. Folks will tend to get a warning for disorderly conduct before they are arrested or issued any paperwork. We just can't go around writing people up for freaking out—or thrashing around. I know you understand this.

The officer was invited into the apartment, where he found the woman responsible for the complaints that had been generated from neighbors and friends. She was a little upset. She admitted that she had been freaking out—and thrashing around. Her reason was reasonable—sometimes reasons can be that way.

The lady had lost her backpack, and within that backpack had been a container that held the ashes of her grandparents. She was thrashing around because she was upset that she couldn't locate it, and she was freaking out for the very same reasons. The officer took into account the reasons for freaking out and thrashing around and he just asked her to try to make a little less noise while she searched. She agreed that she could quiet down.

We do not know if she recovered the container. While we slip into people's lives when asked, we choose to also slip out when we are no longer needed. This is contrary to what many folks believe.

Detroit Dipsticks

The male victim explained that two men had just punched him, smashed his can of Monster Energy drink, and had intentionally broken his prescription sunglasses.

We refer to these as "dirty deeds" in our industry. We do not support it.

The victim's vivid and accurate description of the suspects led the police officer to a couple of men sitting in front of a Main Street emporium specializing in providing high-quality stogies to those who are inclined to smoke.

The two men attempted to do the "I wasn't even there" shuffle as they eased on down the road. If innocently whistling might have helped, they certainly would have done so.

When the officer approached them, one of the men said, "You mother#@%*#rs must be bored up here in Bangor to be f@%*!$g with us!"

The officer—realizing that the man had not attended Father Flanagan's School for Proper Language and Public Etiquette—advised them that he needed to speak to them about a recent assault.

The men refused to give the cop their identification cards.

It should be noted that when you are the suspect in an incident that is under investigation, you must provide identification to police officers. You can continue to refuse, but after a non-specifically determined amount of time, you could go to jail.

The patience of police officers is legendary, but also will vary from state to state. Keep this in mind when you are showing your compadres how it's done. You soon might find that the way "it's done" can often be "no fun." I digress.

The officer was able to gain verifiable suspect identities and determined that both men were under the influence of loudmouth soup, liquid courage, or bottles of instant buffoon (sold and stolen from stores and bars all over the Queen City).

Drinking alcoholic beverages was not permitted in their clearly written bail conditions. It became a problem for one of them who was found to have an active arrest warrant for similar behavior in that lovely city to our south—Portland, Maine.

When the decision was made to take them to jail to end the foul-mouth tirades and vaguely intimidating saliva-spreading salvos of succinctly stupid statements in front of the local children and their guardians, the boys "from away" stepped it up a notch.

One of the boys told the officer that he could "F*&k off." Words can hurt. Name-calling can cause pain, but handcuffs can take the sting out of uncomfortable social situations. We have handcuffs. They are the perfect tool for the introverted police officer who feels uncomfortable during conversations with warrant-laden loudmouths.

The man then told the officer that he was from the City of Detroit, Michigan, and that he was preparing to break the officer in half. We are not saying that it is not possible. We are just saying that this Motor-City Madman was an imposter. He was no Ted Nugent, and he did not fully understand that his personal "Wango Tango" had just begun.

Let's dance!

(The statement, "Let's dance" is written to add a touch of comedic relief to an otherwise tense situation for an officer. We do not say, "Let's dance." We merely do what needs to be done in order to take this type of individual into custody in the quickest, most professional way possible. We always utilize the least amount of force necessary to affect an arrest).

The fight was on, and the potty-mouthed Detroit native was taken into custody after a very, very brief struggle.

A back-up cop stopped by because of the two-bad-guys-one-cop nature of the fracas. We always appreciate a teammate in these situations, and an extra officer was a welcome addition to guide our Michigan marauder into custody. The other man was also placed under arrest for his active arrest warrant.

Don't tell everyone at the jail, but the man was not all that formidable. We hate to share that with other inmates because it takes away from a suspect's "jail-cred." Being the new kid in town (or jail) can cause feelings of inadequacy. These feelings are real, and they were justified in regard to the liquor-laden lads from Detroit.

In this instance, the name of Detroit was used in vain. It was sad for us to witness the sudden demise of the public relations career of the northeastern regional representative of the Motor City.

Detroit boy was charged with Violation of Bail, Assault, Disorderly Conduct, and Refusal to Submit to Arrest.

The other man was arrested on an outstanding arrest warrant and charged with Assault and Criminal Mischief.

It should be noted that the officers were advised by one of the men that his dad is an attorney and that he uses the same attorney as the actor, John Travolta. We cannot confirm this.

We do appreciate the acting skills that Travolta has portrayed in several of his outstanding films. We do not hold him—or his attorney—responsible for any of the antics perpetrated by these two buffoons.

Don't Be Like Bob

On the night before Christmas, we discovered that many creatures were stirring.

Our cops were called to go over to Court Street to speak to a man who was swearing—loudly—at passersby from his vantage point on the front lawn.

The man gave the cops no deference, and upon their arrival in front of his abode, he let them know that they could move along.

He then said that both of them could "F#@* off."

It also appeared that the man had been into the fermented spruce juice that flows freely near Christmas trees all over the world on this holiest of holiday eves.

We've been wished a merry Christmas in many unique ways, but this salutation was like the sharp shard of a peppermint stick driven through all that is holy and bright.

One of the officers asked him his name. The man said, "Bob, and you can still F#@* off." Bob stood in defiance of all that Christmas represented, at least, to us.

A quick look-see into the MBOAW (Merry Bucket of

Arrest Warrants) revealed that Bob had failed to take care of a court date back in November. It was exactly the Christmas miracle that the cops hoped for all season long. Say nothing for all the tenants in Bob's building who just wanted to get a couple of quick winks before the kids got up in a few hours.

Bob was advised that he was now being drafted into the incarcerated army of elves who must wear orange jumpsuits and eat turkey loaf sandwiches on Christmas Day. He was handcuffed by the jolly elves in blue.

Bob was silent, just the way he should have been earlier, but it was too late. Sometimes, it's just too late.

Doo-Doo Deposit Disaster

A fellow who was visiting our local folk music festival didn't utilize a debit card to make use of the automated teller machine. He had just walked by a legion of clean and pleasant plastic Porta Potties, yet he selected the ATM to make a deposit that was extremely personal in nature.

The caretaker of the machine attempted to pull it away from the roaming pooper during the disastrous download, but he was unable to move it as fast as the man was able to move his bowels. The attendant had seen it all, and he was certainly traumatized by the man's method of checking his balance; he leaned right on the ATM.

When officers were called to deal with the man, he admitted that he had seen all the other locations where his "business" would have been accepted, but the powerful feeling came on when he approached the ATM. He did it purposefully, and this is not an acceptable practice, even in the banking industry.

Using Solomon's wisdom, the officers made the man clean up the mess he had just made (I mean that in every way imaginable) and then had the area sprayed down with high-powered hoses and detergents.

They did not summons the man to a court date because he would have had to sign a ticket, and no one was willing to let him use their pen.

Dr. Dre Beatdown

Our officer discovered that singing because you are happy is not always appreciated by others.

A man, who was enjoying the smooth tracks being delivered to his auditory canals by a brand-new pair of Dr. Dre Beats headphones, was attacked by a woman on Kenduskeag Avenue.

The victim, who tends to sing along with the music as he listens, was strolling and unconcerned when he was wildly attacked by a woman who later claimed that his singing annoyed her to the point that she could not stop attacking him.

It's not like the man was singing along with William Shatner's 1978 rendition of Elton John's "Rocket Man" for crying out loud.

At first, she only took his hat and threw it on the ground. He instinctively called her several names that were not complimentary.

This made her angrier, and she struck him in the head and then grabbed his Dr. Dre Beats (which, at that point in time, seemed aptly named) and ran off to a home on Division Street while gripping only the cord.

The man stood, dumbfounded and cord-free, on the sidewalk. He then called us. He relayed his story to the cops, who located the woman in the home where she had sought refuge.

She admitted to the conduct but explained that the victim's singing annoyed her, and she had asked him to stop several times. He was not compliant with her request, so she felt the need to take action.

The officer pointed out that she might have missed the fact that Dr. Dre Beats are high quality headphones. Also, that the point of headphones was to keep musical noises in and outside voices out. In other words, the headphones had done what they were intended to do.

The suspect said that, due to traumatic events in her past, noises like those the man was making caused her to lash out.

The officer did exactly what needed to be done. He charged the woman with both Theft and Assault. He retrieved the man's cord and returned it to him. When the officer did this, he stood up for horrible singers everywhere. He did it for you; he did it for Dr. Dre; and he did it for American karaoke.

The woman told the officer that she would be fleeing the state of Maine immediately. She claimed that she was heading to Massachusetts. This fun fact bothered no one, but the officer acted disappointed, as he felt it was the kind thing to do.

Drunk, with a Side of Stupid

The clerk at a convenience store noted that the man was visibly drunk, and she followed the rule of "no sales to those that are visibly intoxicated." It's a state law. No kidding.

It seems that this law is commonly violated at saloons and whatnot, but I am not a judge. I am merely the purveyor of stories that I believe need to be told.

While we are appreciative of the clerk's attention to detail in trying to keep the public from doing naughty things, the drunk man was not so keen on her response to his slurred speech and glassy eyes. He determined that it was best to engage her in a battle of wits.

What could go wrong? Well, I'll tell you.

His angry voice kicked in and he asked the the woman what she would do if he were to tell her that he was a robber and he wanted all the money in the register. She showed him.

She called the police department. Touché, drunk moron, touché.

While your BAC (Blood Alcohol Content)—by percentage—might have appeared to be higher than your IQ test scores indicate, we believe the BAC might have been responsible for most of the talking.

When the officer arrived, he found the man, sans liquor, walking across the barren parking lot of despair. It is a dry land surrounded by a thirst that cannot be quenched by a conversation with a sober cop.

He was advised that his choice of a conversational icebreaker should be revised in future visits. He was also given a written warning to stay out of the retail establishment for the next 365 days. This will make it much more difficult to quench his thirst or engage in a battle of wits with a woman who found him to be an idiot, and a drunken one at that.

Drunken Vulcan, or "Drulcan"

One of our officers was sent to a local grocery store to speak to a woman about her claims that she was a Vulcan.

She was also naked.

Upon his arrival, he located the intoxicated woman. She told him that she was not following all of the edicts put forth by her probation officer and that she was going to smoke, drink, and strip naked whenever she liked.

After she was re-clothed, she was driven to a location that would deem her fit to be taken to jail, as her probation officer felt it was the most logical thing to do in this most illogical situation.

Spock could have done no better.

Live long and prosper? Yes, but keep your clothes on.

East Side Dipsticks

A nice lady on the east side complained of stomping, singing, and some pretty loud yelling coming down from the apartment that was—unfortunately—situated directly above her own.

Once she complained to the police, the dwellers who made all that noise determined that they would holler out threatening messages to the nice lady who just wanted a little bit of peace and quiet. Some of their garbled threats went so far as cause her to believe that these dipsticks were willing to bring physical harm to her, and possibly her cat.

Like the cat, the cops came back the very next day.

When discussions ensued about the possibility of threatening behaviors, it was discovered that the two attic dwellers had active arrest warrants for other—similar—behavior.

We took that opportunity to remove them from their apartment and gave them a quick tour of their new digs at the county jail. We thanked them for agreeing to be cordial when, and if, they returned to their old apartment building.

It seems that the landlord was displeased once he heard of their threatening behaviors to his favorite tenant.

Word gets around in a small, small town.

Fallen and Can't Get Up

A man actually called to tell us he had fallen, and he couldn't get up. Sure, those words deliver many of us—who grew up in a certain period—back to the late-night commercials that advertised—ad nauseam—an electronic device that will summon help with the push of a button.

The officer who went to the call is more than likely too young to remember the commercials, but he went anyway.

You call, we come. It's our credo.

The man who called for help was completely honest in his description of events. He had gone out to the lawn to enjoy a nightcap of Josè Cuervo tequila. The night lasted longer than his tequila, and when he decided to call it a day, Josè cut the lights. Compadre Cuervo might have also caused some spinning and reeling; the man was down.

The man was now lying on the front lawn of his home, determined to get back inside. Since he lives alone and probably should purchase one of those buttons—or kick out his roommate, Josè—he called the cops.

You call, we come. It's our credo.

The officer found the gentleman right where Josè left him. He was helped to his feet and delivered to his chair inside the house. The officer reported that it was clear that Josè was gone, so the man should be fine after a good long sleep in the recliner.

We checked back later, and all was well.

Cops sometimes are better friends than Cuervo.

Fireball

Our officers arrived at a local hotel after someone reported—to us—that it was overfilled with patrons involved in the loud and excessive display of mirth and merriment.

Their intentions were only for us to warn the unruly patrons to quiet down.

One lady, however—filled with something more than mirth and merriment—was being asked to leave. She refused.

When officers arrived, they could see the woman clearly; she was now on the roof.

Staffers from the front desk advised the cops that the woman had been consuming alcohol or drugs, possibly both.

She had been unreasonably loud, and that's why they had asked her to leave the premises.

The officer's report states, "She was extremely animated and appeared to be under the influence of an unknown substance. (She) made her way off the roof, swinging unsafely and hollering. I noticed a large group gathering in the parking lot to watch her odd behavior."

When the lady made it to the ground, she told the officer that she had not been using narcotics, but that she had been drinking Fireball whiskey.

Officers can sometimes gain clarity about the reason for a person's antics through active questioning. In this case, the officer merely shook his head from side to side and mumbled under his breath, "Fireball."

The woman then ran into the lobby forcing the officer to give chase. He caught her in the vestibule and applied handcuffs. She was booked at the jail for the violation of Criminal Trespass.

Yup, Fireball.

Florida Woman

A woman who was found walking in the road and yelling at motorists was asked to stop with all of her boisterous nonsense and buffoonery.

She took offense to this and turned her attention to the police officer, who then requested that she leave our byways and return to the location from whence she came. She refused.

The police officer asked her for identification as he was preparing to fill out a document that would invite her to speak to a judge about her method of traffic direction and control.

She refused.

She was less pleasant than the typical woman in the road, almost caustic and sour in both manner and demeanor. It can be disheartening.

The lady used foul language as if it were her native tongue, and she gave our officer several false names. The first two names she gave the officer were discovered to belong to women who did not fit her description in any way, shape, or form. Heights and weights were discombobulated to the point that the woman's story became somewhat of a fairy tale. If she had a more pleasant delivery, we might have listened to her for hours. I am sad to report that "pleasant" was not in her repertoire.

After much too long, we found out her actual name. We then discovered that she was from Ft. Lauderdale, Florida. Her shoulder tattoo of a serpent-like creature confirmed her identity, and—we believe—her spirit animal.

She was placed under arrest, and we were soon made aware that some poor sap from Ft. Lauderdale would be driving up to Maine in order to pick her up so that she could winter in a more pleasant climate.

At the same time, we believe our climate will suddenly become more pleasant. Never before were we so pleased to hear that someone we know was going to Florida for the winter. We do not expect to receive a postcard.

Fundred Acre Wood

Our police officers stopped by to speak to a group of men who were hanging around in the parking lot of the Prentiss Woods walking trails, over on Grandview Avenue.

The officers visited for a few minutes before being informed that one man in the group of magnificent conversationalists currently was wanted on—seven—outstanding arrest warrants. It's the kind of thing that stops a good conversation right in its tracks.

As the officers took him into custody, another man who was there, and who had been very quiet, began to speak in loud tones about the fact that his friend had already taken care of most of his outstanding warrants.

That same man became boiling angry, and he began to speak in a truculent manner. When he was asked to give us his name, he refused to provide it.

The sad news is that the visible tattoo of a revolver—that once seemed like a marvelous idea—now aided the cops in identifying the man without the need for him to give up his name.

It was soon found out that revolver man had two outstanding arrest warrants. Since we already had a car headed to the jail, we were able to economize and put both men in the same car for the short ride to their newly selected hangout spot.

Gaming Loudly

Our officer silently stood outside the door where the distur-bance was taking place. It was quiet for a few minutes, but then someone yelled again. The cop knocked.

A young man answered the door and told the peace offi-cer that there was no one else in the home. This could not be true; he had heard it for himself. He needed to investigate. The young man asked the lawman to come in and take a look around.

Once inside, the officer found no one else. He was sure he had heard a female hollering. When the officer noticed the headphone and microphone set attached to the gaming con-sole, he began to piece it all together.

The young man *did* have a rather high-pitched voice; our cop inquired if the young man was playing *Fortnite*. The lad admitted that he was and that he was losing badly. He admit-ted to screaming, "Get off me," several times while he was under attack in the game.

Our Blue Squire was not required to become a High-Rise Assault Trooper in this instance. While the Venturion had the voice of a Ventura, he was merely passionately involved in gaming—we get it. (No, we really don't.)

The lad was warned to keep it down. He said he would.

Granite State Madman

The police officer that arrived on-scene in front of the pub was alarmed to find a man lying face down on the sidewalk.

A colorful sign, set up on the sidewalk to advertise a couple of drink specials and promote one beer over another, was lying nearby.

It appeared that in a fit of something or other, the man—who was later found to be from New Hampshire—had heaved the sign at the pub window. This far-flung—now aeronautical—advertising sign bounced off the window and struck the native New Hampster directly, knocking him over and causing him some discomfort in the form of a lump on his noggin.

Able-bodied paramedics were treating the pummeled laureate, who was found to be from the northern regions of the Granite State.

Later, at the hospital, the man—now conscious—admitted to throwing the sign, but he could not recall why he would do such a thing.

Some nearby participants in this boozy ballet that ended

badly—who were believed to be employed in the field of medicine and healing—whispered to the man something about his blood-alcohol levels. It was only then that he slowly shook his head up and down as if to indicate to those surrounding him that he now understood that those levels were higher than those of men who had not previously partaken of spirits.

In essence, the New Hampster threw the sign in a fit of drunken fun, and it came back to bite him. This "bite"—in the form of a strike—toppled the Granite Stater so as to introduce his melon to our granite sidewalks. Pain and bedazzlement ensued. He would be fine if he took two aspirin and called someone in the morning, just as long as it was not us.

We moved on after giving him a summons for damaging the pub's property. The sign—we were told—belonged to the beer company. It was remarkably undamaged in the affair. It was stood back up more easily than the man who'd traveled here from an adjacent land that is also reported to be filled with moose and bear.

We suspect they also have moose and beer. That means that the New Hampster should be able to nurse his wounds and tell his story at a pub in that locale. He can someday share a parable about that time he went to Bangor and discovered that their granite was equal to any found in the land of those who want to "Live Free or Die."

Healthcare Mayhem

A visitor to a facility charged with healing the sick came unhinged when they were not attended to in a manner they felt was appropriate. The person claimed that during a past visit they had been treated in the same way.

We get it. On one occasion—in the cafeteria of that same facility—I was informed that they no longer served chocolate shakes. I became enraged. I kept it bottled up inside, and it manifested as a smile when I vented my anger by going with vanilla and using two straws instead of the standard one straw.

The straws are constructed from paper, and not plastic, so relax a little bit.

The person made verbal threats about breaking things, and—a short time later—several items in the room were found to have been destroyed. This is not acceptable in modern society, but it seems like a trend. Trends become all too common, and that makes us sad.

Our officer went to survey the damage. The individual who had made the statements now claimed that they must have tripped on their way to the bathroom.

In the same way that your mother knew you were lying, we can sometimes determine that a person might be spreading untruths. Since the (now demolished) television had been mounted to a wall about seven feet from the well-polished floor, and the person was well under five-feet-nine-inches tall, the officer felt strongly that something was missing from the person's storyline.

It would take more than just a leap—even if it were to be a leap based on faith alone—in order to bust up the flat-screen boob tube that was lag-bolted to the amazingly sanitary ceiling.

Utilizing the most basic physics, guesstimating by the amount of damage to the television, and noticing that the pathway to the bathroom in no way intersected with the location where the Samsung had previously hung, the officer determined that someone was lying.

I should also share that one advantage to having a private room at a healthcare facility is that there are very few suspects who need to be interviewed for us to conclude an investigation of this magnitude.

We could not prove or disprove their statement, so the individual was charged with criminal mischief and then advised that they could tell their story to the judge.

We can only hope that the judge is on time for the proceedings. We find that—sometimes—their timeliness is not next to their Godliness. Judges tend to be unaccepting of this premise. I mean, except for the Godliness part.

Herbal Fury

An individual who walked into a tea and tobacco store felt the need to comparison shop for rolling papers. It was presumably to be used to inhale either tobacco smoke or another plant-based herbal remedy.

The clerk, well-versed in selling such wares, showed the man his current stock of items designed to comfortably burn one or two.

The habitué of herbal highs hedged at the hoard of hemp papers. His personality did not reflect the calm and peaceful mood that the clerk hoped his helpfulness would habituate. Instead, the shopper lashed out and began to drop f-bombs in the manner of a man who needed to be rolled into a really big group hug.

The man did not think that the papers presented were appropriate for the proprietor of a pot-paper emporium and continued to display his displeasure in a very derogatory diatribe.

The perturbed paper seeker began to push the proprietor, physically, not metaphorically. The now-displeased shopkeeper requested that the man leave the store immediately.

This caused the shopper to call the man a four-letter word for Richard (hint: not Rich) and become angrier and more volatile.

The seething seeker of paper products then told the clerk that he was going to "F@*k him up," and the fight was on.

He swung at the clerk, and the clerk made moves "like Jagger," which caused his attacker to fall upon the floor. I would have used the term "zigged and zagged," but it would have been too easy, and I hate to go for the cheap jokes.

As the man became supine on the floor, the clerk felt it best to make sure he stayed down until police arrived. He continued to use physical force to keep the man down and at the same time he dialed 9-1-1 for some reinforcement from the Bangor Police Department. The Illinois National Guard would have taken far too long.

The patron—now with a bloody nose and no smoking papers—got up and ran from the store. The result of his bad decisions caused droplets of his life-sustaining fluids to mark his direction of travel. The man was headed south, in the general direction of McDonald's.

My dad always told me, "Son, if you get in trouble, run toward McDonald's." We never discussed why, but I have to tell you, I have been fighting the few extra pounds most of my life. I digress.

We never found the man. We suspect he reverted to a pipe for all of his smoking needs.

Hot Balls

In late July, a couple of our police officers were alarmed to hear that a man was reported to have arrived at the back door of a local shelter. He was yelling incessantly about the pain he was currently experiencing.

Now, you might believe that calling an ambulance was in order, and it was. However, the man took off running into the night as quickly as he arrived.

The gathering of specific details is imperative in our job. The officers went to speak to witnesses who then added a few spicy details to the short snippets of information they had received from professional and competent late-night dispatchers.

It seems the reason the man was screaming in pain was— he claimed—because he had been sprayed in his very own short snippets by a person who had excellent aim with a can of pepper spray.

Pepper spray can really sting when sprayed directly in the eyes, but this man had received his dose in an area where pepper spray is not intended to be applied.

For most of us, the wearing of shirts, pants, and other essentials is one of the things that protect us from being doused in the private places by a pepper-wielding perp. The fact that this man was completely naked makes it all the more clear that being appropriately dressed is important if you go out carousing after dark.

The cops found the man easily. His cries of pain carried quite well from the wooded area where he was nursing his spiced berries with the cool condensation that tends to linger on the leaves of oaks and maples as the darkness allows the greenery to cool after the summer sun sets—late—on a Maine July evening.

We do not suggest utilizing any foliage from our state tree—the white pine—as it can be sticky, and it stings a bit when rubbed the wrong way.

When the man finally emerged, one kind shelter staff member offered him a pitcher of cold milk to be applied to his warm spots with the intent of mitigating some of the effects of the residual pepper that was stuck to his p@#$*r.

He eschewed the milk, nary even taking a sip to take his mind off the burning. He was questioned about how he happened to be naked, sprayed, and running. The cops felt there must be more to the story. He refused to give any information about the dilemma that drove him to seek respite for his twig and berries.

He was offered medical care, and he refused that as well. He claimed he would go home and just wait it out.

Of course, a story like this would never be made into a television series. Who is going to watch unclothed humans attempting to survive the elements with no help from the outside world?

"Naked and Sprayed" is just too silly of a title to offer up to the producers of reality television programs. I'll try to think of something else.

In the Pants Stuff

A man at a State Street convenience store was confronted by the clerk regarding the large supply of Natty-Daddy malt liquor cans that he was stuffing down his pants. They were cold and full.

The man agreed to retrieve the cans and began to pull them out one by one. In the process, the clerk noticed that the man had also secreted away a bag of Cape Cod kettle-cooked potato chips. I will attest that I find these chips a delicious treat. Well, not those specific chips, but Cape Cod chips in general.

As soon as the man harvested all the cans and snacks, he was permitted to leave with no charges. This was the choice of the management.

As the officers left the store, they were dispatched to attend to a similar complaint at another convenience store within easy walking distance from the first.

Upon their arrival, they were not surprised to find the same man now removing six cans of Natty from his pants. At this location, he had also stolen a Fast Break candy bar. Salty and sweet took on a whole new meaning for our crew.

He was charged for the second theft, but he was only summoned and not taken to jail.

We cannot say for sure, but it is possible that the officers did not want to be responsible for a search of the man's person. Any individual who can secure that many canned goods in his basement is certainly likely to be carrying much more in his closets.

Kevin

A man named Kevin was relieving himself on our downtown sidewalk after spending a night on the town.

Several out-of-town police officers were walking by when Kevin suddenly turned and sprayed them with a liquid formerly known as beer.

This full-screen showing also caused Kevin to flash them a full-frontal view of his "southern-dwelling gentleman."

Kevin slurred an attempted apology, but his vocalized congeniality divided his attention enough so that he continued to rotate toward them as they tried to scurry away.

In a deluge that could be similar to that created by a large African elephant as it jubilantly sprays a cooling mist on its friends at the watering hole, Kevin had a tremendous capacity for both holding—and expending—fluid.

If Kevin had been a mortarman in the United States military, his aim would have drawn accolades from all his superior officers. These officers were unimpressed, but still shellshocked, by his incessant and steady stream.

In this case, his laser-like aim and fuzzy focus merely

soaked the lower pant legs of one of the out-of-towners who—now—seemed less likely to come back to our pleasant city on the river. When I say, "the river," I am talking about the Penobscot River and not the amber stream that Kevin had created right on our clean concrete walkways.

It was unfortunate—for Kevin—that there were a few ladies present for his show. They made a complaint about the forced review of the man's twig and walnuts, and we had no choice but to charge Kevin for indecent conduct.

Keyboard in the Pants

Shoplifting is sometimes referred to as a victimless crime. We disagree.

One of our finest was sent to a local big-box retailer that is known for value pricing on everything from refrigerators to flat-screen televisions.

It is a place where the staff smiles—sometimes condescendingly—at your lack of knowledge about requirements for RAM, your perplexed stare when they are speaking of pixels, and certainly the silliness that you present when you ask for a Samsung rather than the iPhone 12. It is the nature of the game, and they must be smug when dealing with mere mortals who have come to their domain to be electronically entertained; we get it.

In this case, they called us. Apparently, a man had entered, stolen, and then vanished into the night in the cab of a late-model Silverado. They needed the cops.

The man in question had been able to unbox a very high-end keyboard. However, the term "high-end" is relative when speaking of an item that was smuggled out of the store in the back of a man's pants.

I know what you are thinking, how can a keyboard be unboxed inside the store? I know that just the vault-like plastic packaging on my last replacement television remote left me battered and bleeding after a two-to-three-hour cage match that included edged weapons and the utilization of a vice. No, not vice grips, a vice.

If my previous stable of remotes had been made from the same material as that packaging, I wouldn't have to spend so much time in the big electronics store having my knowledge of flat-screen technology questioned by a youngster who was dropped off at work by his mother. Not because he couldn't get his own driver's license, but merely because his mother is tired of being corrected and advised to unplug it, then plug it back in. She drops him off so she can just be home, alone, for a break from hearing the microwave running incessantly while he cooks Hot Pockets. I apologize for getting off-topic.

The man stole the keyboard by taking it out of the packaging and then secreting it away in the tight confines of his personal packaging.

We looked at the parking lot camera footage and found that it was all but useless for a good description because the cameras "need to be updated." Well-played, blue-vested geniuses, well-played.

We were told by security that, "the man didn't even walk

funny" as he sauntered away, unconcerned with their prying eyes. They could have used some private eyes. We believe that what they would have seen would have caused a severe burning sensation.

While we did not catch him, we cannot help but wonder if the company that built that keyboard might be interested in what level of humidity the components had to survive in order to be plugged-in—and working well—at its final destination.

Could it have been stolen as a gift? Did he steal a can of compressed air to blow out detritus left behind (see what I did there) from transportation and sub-level storage?

The root of the story is that we didn't catch him, and he has a new three-hundred-dollar keyboard.

I wonder, late at night, if he ever hits the shift key and considers that the word—pre-printed on all keyboards—could be misspelled. I mean, at least on this particular keyboard.

Kicking the Ass of the Trashman

A man who reportedly threatened to "kick the @##" of the trashman was pulled back into the house by a spouse who found his behavior problematic.

The trashman had—apparently—left several bags of trash behind when he moved forward to the next driveway on his route. This made the man somewhat angry, and he vented. He first loudly inquired why the refuse had been refused.

The guy who was guiding the garbage truck made it clear that there was a five-bag limit on pick-up, and he couldn't take any more bags. This infuriated the man who was left holding the bag—a couple of bags, really.

That's when the words became heated, and opening a (garbage) can of whoop-@## was about to become a reality show. Threatening words are never the answer to an overflowing trashcan. But tempers tend to flare when the remnants of Friday fish night are forced to stay at your place for the foreseeable future. It's infuriating.

The truck driver called his dispatch center; they called the cops; and we were all thankful that the man's wife acted as the control rod that only the lady of the house can do so well.

Only verbal warnings for the verbal warriors were necessary. Reuse, Recycle, and Reply Kindly are edicts that should not be discarded. These times are stressful.

Killing for Satan

One of the rights of passage for a young police officer is the day they are first sent to contend with an issue involving Satan.

There is no specific course work in the police academy where Beelzebub is brought up—by name—in conversation. The Prince of Darkness is never mentioned when we talk about the titles and sections of state statutes or during the training regarding the mechanics of arrest, restraint, and control.

A person who spends their life on the outskirts of police work might only have to contend with a mention of Satan on certain Sundays as they worship freely in the church of their choosing.

Our house of worship is open 24/7/365, usually only closing for the cleaning of the bathrooms; there are times where even that is a stretch.

Certainly, everyone has heard terminology about "Giving the Devil his due," or singing about the day when "The Devil went down to Georgia." But cops tend to find at least one person per year who claims to have more intimate knowledge, maybe even a deeply harbored hatred, in regard to the boss of the deep underworld.

Cops were sent to a call where a male voice was heard screaming repeatedly that he was, "going to kill for Satan." Now, just digesting the words might lead you to believe that if a person is truly ready to kill for Lucifer, he or she won't have much problem killing anyone who gets in the way of their mission. So sometimes that kind of chatter is similar to the old adage about idle hands.

Thus, calls to homes where they are giving loud shout-outs—to the devil—will cause you to temper the speed of your entry into those abodes. We tend to wade into that pool a little more slowly than you might during other calls for service where Satan isn't mentioned at all.

Upon their arrival, the man in question—wearing only tighty whities—admitted that much of his well-vocalized aggravation was due to a recent and unexpected eviction notice. It was discovered during an amicable conversation that the man had a couple of active arrest warrants as well. He mentioned that additional stress was added to his boiling cauldron of anger when he lost the key to his front door while out for a walk. We didn't inquire if he had taken off his pants before, or after, the walk mainly because we didn't need to know. Actually, we didn't want to know.

The man admitted that his outburst was unnecessary and apologized loudly to his neighbors so they could hear him through the walls. He also admitted that threatening to kill for the Devil was just a silly way to vent. We told him we fully understood.

Oddly, the man's arrest warrants were for failure to appear. We are happy to report that this was also the case in regard to Mephistopheles.

He was taken to jail. We left the door ajar so that he could get back in once he was released from the county.

Last Fumes from
an Empty Gas Tank

An officer who was patrolling on Griffin Road was waved down by a man who had run out of gas.

The officer is neither a smoker, a joker, or a midnight toker, but he is a helper. He told the troubled man that he would call for another officer to come to their location so there was enough manpower to push the truck into the parking lot of a nearby mall.

The second cop arrived, and they pushed the truck while the owner steered. As progress slowed, the man left the cab and ran back to help the two officers push the pick-up.

Many hands make light work, but steering is important. The truck veered suddenly to the left, and the car owner asked one of the officers to grab the wheel and steer toward the parking area. The officer complied with the regretful request, and when he opened the door to access the wheel, he saw what could never again be unseen.

Four baggies containing a suspicious white powder were

in the footwell of the truck. The officer, who does not play poker on a regular basis, kept his smirk to himself and his eyes on the road as he corrected the trajectory of the pick-up truck filled with what appeared to be Peruvian marching powder. We believe he might have snickered a bit, for it felt good to be alive.

All hands were needed to keep this coke-fueled mule train running, and the cop returned to the tailgate with a re-newed sense of vim and vigor. The operator took the wheel again, and they made it into the parking space.

If you close your eyes and concentrate, you might be able to hear the giggles of delight that happened just before the truck stopped and the driver returned to the tailgate to thank the officers for their service.

The officer confronted the man about his cargo and the warm feelings of camaraderie slipped away like the last fumes from an empty gas tank. The man admitted to buying the co-caine just before he ran out of fuel.

His admission came with the caveat that he felt that he might have been ripped off by his dealer because he was not feeling the effects of the line of "coke" he had snorted prior to meeting up with the po-po.

The officer used a field-testing kit, and the powder was found to be something other than cocaine. This confirmed that the man did not get what he paid for. He looked disap-pointed and relieved. That's a difficult look to pull-off.

There must be a lesson here somewhere, but the good news is that there were no charges available for buying fake cocaine or running out of gasoline. Both tasks take a certain level of competence, and the man appeared to have been shorted in all areas related to that.

The man thanked the officers for the push, and the confirmation that he had purchased something other than cocaine. He told the cops that their kindness had left him with a much more positive impression of police.

Lay-Out

On Sunday night, Bangor police were called to check a Garland Street address for a man who was lying on the front lawn of a home.

Our terminology, in Bangor, for this activity is a "lay-out." We know that it is not grammatically correct, but we suppose, silently, that a man lying drunk on a front lawn is not all that concerned about grammar.

It can be cold many nights of the year and intentionally sleeping on a lawn without shelter, or even a ground cloth, does raise an eyebrow or two. In the officer's case, his proper grooming techniques have kept his eyebrows non-connected, so he raised both of them.

The man said he was resting there and was in search of female companionship. This caused one of the officer's eyebrows to drop slightly in a very Belushi-esque manner.

To be upfront, the man on the lawn did not describe his search for ladies in such a polite way, and we know that if he used similar terminology while courting our local damsels, he would soon be seeking the help of a doctor and a dentist. We have some great practitioners here in Bangor.

Our cops asked the gentleman to get off the lawn and move along. He complied. We do not know if he was able to locate a companion.

They say there is a match for every person. During times like these, we tend to believe otherwise.

Maine Moose Moss

A local gentleman reported that someone had kicked in his door and stolen half an ounce of his marijuana while he was out on the town.

Upon the arrival of the officer, the man upgraded the amount of the missing chill-spinach to one whole ounce. We assume he had done a complete inventory of the stash during the time between the call and the arrival of the po-po.

One thing you need to remember is that it is tough for us to add the appropriate value for your personal provisions when filling out our reports. While we estimated the value at about $150, he swore it was of the highest quality and that he had paid "his guy" much more than that.

We can only use data from reliable sources such as price-ofweed.com for our reports. Please be aware of this if you are reporting stolen weed and have somehow lost or misplaced your receipt for same.

It came to light that the man who'd had his special herb diabolically diverted, had recently come home drunk. He was bragging to friends about kicking in his own door instead of utilizing more common methods such as keys and the door-knob.

This revelation cast doubt on much of his story, but we cannot be the judge and jury. We are merely the men and women who document daily dalliances with doors, dope, drinks, and doses of dumb-assery.

It was determined that if he had "forgotten" that his door was already smashed, he could have been "mistaken" about where his Maine-made magic moose moss had gone.

He was advised to notify the landlord and to make sure he shared that he had caused at least some of the damage on his own.

These times do try us.

McChicken Sandwich

A gentleman sitting in a running automobile in a parking lot had apparently passed out behind the wheel. Passersby made the call to our department.

The officer who walked up to the car saw that the gear selector was in the D position.

D refers to Drive if you want to move forward. In this case, it could have stood for Drunk. The odor of intoxicating beverages wafted out from the open window.

The officer also noticed—that sitting in the man's lap—there was a half-eaten McChicken sandwich in its original yellow wrapping paper. The insignia indicating that it came from the Golden Arches was clearly visible as it was emblazoned on the paper.

The lump of mayonnaise in the man's hair told us a story that he wouldn't otherwise share.

The man did say that he had just come from a restaurant where he had picked up his dinner. Sadly, when he was asked where he picked up his dinner, the man told the officer that he'd gotten it at Pizza Hut.

In our line of work, a statement like that is referred to as a clue.

The man was offered the chance to take a few field sobriety tests, but he refused. He was taken to jail. No pizza boxes were found at the scene.

Meat in Pants

A man who appeared to be a connoisseur of fine, well-marbled beef found exactly what he was looking for at one of our clean and convenient grocery emporiums.

The man did not specify to the officer that he had researched the proper aging of the beef, but our cops are almost certain that stuffing the meat down your pants does not follow the simple rule of keeping the meat in "a cool and dry place."

Our cop is not a butcher, a baker, or a candlestick maker. He is a cop. He was thankful that the fine Angus beef loins had been retrieved from the man's loins before his arrival to deal with the rare (see what I did there?) occurrence.

A quick review of the man's recent activity revealed that he had used this method of masterful meat management and manipulation in the not-so-distant past. Just the week before, he had done the same thing at another store.

Armed with this information, the cop decided to arrest the man and take him to the county jail (where steak was not served that night) to answer to a judge the following morning. After washing his hands, our officer got back to the grind.

Moment of Weakness with the Star Land Vocal Band

A man called the police department and reported that his former girlfriend was inside his apartment and she was deeply engrossed in the age-old sport of throwing things at him.

It sounded to our competent dispatcher that the woman was throwing things as the man continued to speak on the phone.

Dispatchers are very in tune with the nuances of a relationship gone bad, and in this case, the loud thuds and smashing glass were more than subtle nuances; she expedited a couple of cops to the scene.

Upon their arrival, the woman had run out of objects to throw, even after recycling a couple of items for a second go-around. She was tired.

The man was none worse for the wear. He explained that her aim was poor and he had been able to dodge most of the items that had been drafted to be utilized as missiles and fodder.

The man informed the cops that his ex-girlfriend had a court order in effect that made it illegal for her to have any contact with him. The next question is obvious to all of us, and, even to you, the reader.

How did the ex-girlfriend end up in the man's apartment?

The man explained that he had contacted her to come over in what he described as "a moment of weakness." The two had engaged in some physical contact, and it was then made clear to the cops that she had since stolen his wallet, keys, and his electronic benefits card.

Judging by the condition of the apartment, our cops were under the impression that these must have been the only three things that she did not throw at the man.

The suspect admitted to all of it, probably more so because it was hard to deny. She was arrested after the officers found that she did have active bail conditions that banished her from the apartment or from having any contact with the man.

While en route to the jail, the woman complained of some chest pain. She said that it was clear that she was having a heart attack.

Regardless of the fact that the woman had displayed a tireless effort in throwing very heavy things with no obvious signs of even the least bit of fatigue or pain, the cops rushed her to the emergency room. Competent medical attention was quickly provided by those who are trained as physicians. Even they were disheartened to learn that she was "faking it." She admitted it after tests proved it, and she was delivered to the jail to be held for the charges.

The victim might have requested restitution for the damage to his apartment, but that would be for the courts to decide. In my opinion, if his motto has always been "when it's right it's right" when asking for a little afternoon delight, he should have expected some skyrockets in flight. Just saying.

More Loud Lovemaking

We have no idea what has been added to the water supply, but our officers were recently called to a west-side neighborhood. The caller complained of ongoing, loud lovemaking at a nearby residence.

The legalities of libidinous activity are well documented, but let me lay it out for you: There is no law against love or the making of same.

When we are called to intercede in the amatory pursuits of the citizenry, it typically is only because things have become publicly uproarious.

Sure, we urge you to get a room, but also shut the windows, turn on a noisy fan, or crank some Van Halen.

Please mitigate so that we don't need to litigate.

It should be noted, and well documented, that we really don't see our role as the gatekeepers of "getting it on." However, if your lascivious late-evening forays into fornication force us to start knocking, please make sure the van stops rocking.

I say all this to tell you that when we did knock, one of

the parties to the party answered the door. That person indicated that the escapades had ceased for the evening and that there would be no more noise.

Officers wandered away, unconcerned about returning, as we know it is far better to make love, not war.

Could This Have Been Mrs. McGillicuddy?

Our contingent of professional officers at Bangor International Airport made the pages of "Got Warrants." Stalwart defenders of air safety from the TSA discovered that a woman was concealing liquor on her person and trying to get on a jet to travel somewhere south of here.

I say "somewhere south of here" only because none of the planes that leave Bangor are headed somewhere north of here.

I have been petitioning for a flight to Canada for years. I have always been told the same thing: Why would you fly when it would probably take less time to walk? Valid point.

Back to our liquor-laden lady traveler. If the woman had only tried to get one bottle of liquor onboard the plane, we would have ignored this story completely. What officials discovered was that the lady had taped several containers of Dr. McGillicuddy Mentholmint Schnapps to her ankles.

This caused them to check her person in a more thorough manner. They discovered five more mini-bottles taped to her back, under a back brace. A total of nine bottles of the elixir were found in various places on her body. Dr. McGillicuddy gets around; that's what I have heard.

The saddest part of being subjected to the search was that the woman could have legally and comfortably carried the tiny bottles through the checkpoint without losing any skin cells from the requisite peeling of the tape.

She said she did not like the prices of liquor in airports or planes and had not realized that she could BYOBITB (Bring Your Own Booze in Tiny Bottles) while traveling by air.

After further confirmation that it was only Dr. McGillicuddy Mentholmint, she was allowed to fly out of BIA.

The report indicates that "all the bottles were tested and found not to be a threat." I do not have any information on test methods.

I can confirm that for the first time ever, all the folks at the checkpoint appeared happy.

Naked on the Bridge
Over the River, Why?

Two males crossed streams while crossing the stream. Yes, it's physically possible.

Downtown Bangor hosted a couple of purveyors of pee when they were caught with their pants down on the Franklin Street Bridge. The thing is, they stood on the rail rather than trying to be discrete from the street. I get it.

Proudly peeing from a perch presents non-participants with a clear view of all that God gave you.

Participating in post-hydration precipitation is sometimes a predicament that overwhelms our ability to pinch it off. Perfectly placed pee perturbs the perch, brings embarrassment to the eels, and even the inmates—peering out the portholes of the county jail—are pretty much put out with watching prison television programming. How many times can you watch *The Price Is Right*?

Tinkling on turtles could be considered way too much, but turtles never tattle. Too bad the lady who was strolling by couldn't have just turned away. Instead, she called the cops.

We went, but only because the men did first.

When asked why they couldn't wait, one of the men said that pandemic restrictions at portable potties had placed them off limits to people with prostate trouble. We got to the bottom of it all.

Instead of getting our panties all up in a bunch, cops warned the men to go forth and pee no more. At least from the top of the bridge rail.

Prouder moments have been seen on Franklin Street, but at least they didn't pee on the seat.

Nick

A man—called Nick—was kicked out of a downtown watering hole. He was not pleased by the way his night had ended.

He became angry as he approached the exit door. This is sometimes the point where common sense and an alcoholic stupor converge to create a vortex of bad decisions.

Nick did not have the fortitude to resist the vortex.

He suddenly became angry and said that he was not leaving. It was at this point in time that Nick began to overuse the F-bomb. Screams of "eff this" and "eff that" sucked the joy right out of the room.

It was clear to all the patrons that this wasn't Saint Nick, that's for sure.

Nick was offered other options, with jail being only one of many.

The officer felt that if Nick had been given a list of all the possible choices, written in bold black letters, he would have pointed to the word jail. Every. Single. Time.

Nick was thick.

He then determined that he would provoke those who warned him of his impending ride to the jail. Nick took to loud threats of physical violence to all who dared remove him from the drained and upended glasses that created a—not so nice—Nick at night.

Nick was arrested without incident. The streets became a more pleasant place to be once Nick went night-night.

No Nuggets

A man, upset because his twenty-piece chicken nugget package was not in his bag after arriving at his home, returned to and re-entered a fast-food emporium simply to berate the staff.

While this might seem like a dire situation, it gets worse. He also did not get the extra sauce that he ordered.

We have determined through focus groups and studies of other nugget users that being angry about missing condiments when, in fact, the only reason you ordered the extra condiments was that you were expecting to use those condiments on the originally ordered items, which were also not found in the bag, is both unnecessary and creates unwanted negativity in your life.

The theory was proven when the man became aggressive and extremely discourteous to management and staff. Children, who were nearby partaking in similar foods with a maturity level that defied their years, watched in awe as this adult avoided "adulting."

The nugget-less man used foul and coarse language and

made threatening statements. The manager's co-worker—also her twin—jumped in to protect the lady with whom she shared both genes and, on occasion, jeans.

The words, "Not my sister, not today," were not heard, but were imagined, as we would never even think about taking on twins over some missing deep-fried dead chicken and high-fructose-corn-syrup–filled nugget-nectar decanters.

While the sudden appearance of the twin probably made the man believe he was in a re-make of the McMatrix, he did not slow his roll.

A local bouncer—known to occasionally kick the nuggets out of others when they become too drunk and boisterous—decided that he might be needed to intervene. His presence brought a calm to the man never seen since the day he discovered that you could get ten nuggets for a buck at a competing restaurant chain that is *not* within reasonable walking distance of his lair.

The cops arrived; the man became even calmer, and he was issued a criminal trespass warning for the next twelve months.

The next year is now going to be referred to as the "TYONN," or "The Year Of No Nuggets."

It should also be noted that the restaurant, despite his bad behavior, gave the man a full order of nuggets and plenty of sauces for his trouble.

Our officers gave him a ride home. We don't hold

grudges, and we were going that way anyway. For the record, he offered us no nuggets.

In a world full of unkindness, be the person who is big enough to still provide sustenance—and a ride—to known detractors of your nuggets and sauce.

North Dakota Man

A man from North Dakota disappointed many other men from North Dakota when he was seen running from a local grocery store after he stole a bottle of alcohol.

He was described as tall, white, and wearing a dark jacket, a green shirt, and tan pants. None of the aforementioned attributes or descriptors were all that disappointing. He dressed just as any man from Maine, or North Dakota, might dress.

When he was spotted skulking along a fence line, our cops yelled out for him to stop and come back; he didn't.

It should be noted that we don't really expect you to come back when we yell, but we also like to provide a bit of dramatic flair just before we break into a foot chase with any suspect.

Interestingly enough, our cop yelled out, "You are not free to leave!" Frankly, and to be perfectly honest, he actually was free to leave if he chose to do so since he was so far away when the cop yelled.

The chosen phraseology sounds so much better than, "Don't run, because we don't want to chase anyone right now!"

He ran.

The cops chased him, and they soon resorted to lines like, "Stop! Police!" They also just said things like, "Stop," without adding the word, "Police" directly after it. That was mostly because they were out of breath and it had nothing to do with the fact that they were withholding important information from the man.

We are firm believers in the saying that most American fathers utilized as their credo up until the mid to late 1990s: "We really should only have to tell you one time."

When the man tripped on a set of concrete stairs, we were able to take him into custody. This was certainly not the way it happens on television.

The man had stolen a bottle of 1792 bourbon and it appeared that several servings had been surreptitiously sipped sometime during the shenanigans.

He provided the cops with a photo license from the state of North Dakota. He also told them, "This is a felony for me, I have a lot of priors." This is not the point where men from North Dakota will be disappointed. Neither is the fact that the man told our cops that he stole the bottle—now de-capped— with the full intention of trading it for a bit of giggle smoke. That is to say, marijuana.

None of this should bring shame to North Dakota. The disappointment was that the man told us that the reason he was drunk had nothing to do with his few sips of 1792.

No, the part that we know may disappoint some of his North Dakota brethren is that he admittedly had consumed a bottle and a half of stolen chardonnay, and it wasn't even chilled.

We are sorry that you had to hear it from us, especially if you hail from Fargo, Devil's Lake, Larimore, or even Gwinner.

This will not bode well for the plans for an impromptu prodigal son's parade when the man is extradited back to Bismarck for his outstanding arrest warrants.

Drinking stolen and non-chilled Chardonnay is *not* "North Dakota nice!"

Our cops did not know—at the time—that the man was from North Dakota. Nor did they know that even South Dakota men, from as far away as Rapid City, or even Deadwood, would also be disappointed in the man.

Not a Yeti

A woman on the east side of the city called us for police assistance. She rightfully claimed that a man outside in the middle of the street was screaming obscenities.

She said that as she watched from her window, the man walked into her yard and began to beat on her house in the manner that a Yeti might. That is, if that Yeti believed that the knocking might bring him some female companionship, or get him noticed enough to actually be caught on camera by someone who continuously claimed he was real during late-night postings in chatrooms on the Interweb.

No one claims he was a Yeti, and I am merely trying to draw attention to the wonderfully forested areas that surround Bangor, Maine. Once known as the Lumber Capital of the World, Bangor has in recent years been known more as the location where drunken foreigners are dropped off when they act up on passenger jets coming—and going—from the UK and other European hotspots.

Bangor Police are called several times a year to help in the removal of these soccer fans, and they are usually more sober and amicable by the time they realize they have been dropped off in one of the coldest spots in America. It makes us giggle, because they are usually dressed for their planned destinations. Florida is a favorite, but the Caribbean and Mexico are where these folks want to be. "Flip-flop" is a term we use when making buckwheat pancakes—for Yetis. I digress.

The man who was banging on the house of the lady was reported to have been sporting gray hair and wearing a green-and-black buffalo-plaid woolen—or flannel—shirt. She claimed he appeared to be drunk.

This description does not help us much in locating a specific individual. This description is the uniform of the day in most of central northern eastern Maine. I am not saying that all Mainers are drunk, or that they always wear plaid. As a person from away, you might note that this is a commonly held belief. Sadly, it is possible that you are not wrong. There are days when we wear other plaids, however. Don't try to put us in a box.

The cop found the man wandering on the next street over. The man was drunk, wearing plaid, and screaming—still—like a Yeti. Our officer only asked him to quiet down, and stay out of people's yards. He asked for some photo identification, in order to clear better-behaved Yetis who might frequent our city.

The man produced a piece of unopened mail, pointing to the name and address on the envelope. He claimed it was all he had to prove to us who he was. Confirmation of the information was quickly dispensed from our competent dispatchers. The plaid-clad man was asked to quiet down and wander home as soon as possible. No mention was made of our Yeti concerns since we actually laid our eyes on this suspect. Even a simple cop knows that Yetis don't wear bright flannel and carry mail in their pockets. It would be silly to think so.

Nunchuck Warrior

A motorist who had no idea that Bruce Lee might have been reincarnated as a local motorcyclist called our agency to report that she had run into an overzealous two-wheeled ninja warrior.

She was clear and concise when she complained—rightfully so—about a scooterist who was acting aggressively. She told the officer that the rider she encountered had pulled out a set of nunchucks and began swinging them at her automobile as he passed her, flailing the device, at a rapid pace.

She did not know what brand of motorcycle the man was riding, but we picture it as a flat-black Ural. Most of the Russian-built Urals would never run long enough to make it to the movie theater. We believe that if the motorcyclist was a reasonably functional mechanic, he could operate it locally for short periods of time. This explains why he had not spent more time training in the weapons related to martial arts; someone had to keep the bike running. Rumor has it that he is still searching for his 10mm socket. I digress.

The rider—turned POD (Presenter of Dipsticks)—was

not as adept at swinging the weapon as Bruce Lee would have been. The swinger of sticks—connected by cordage—missed her fender completely. That footage would never make the sizzle reel for a really good end-of-times motor-centric thriller.

Our cop did not see the original *Mad Max* movie because his parents were only ten and eleven years old in 1979. Seeing Mel Gibson enraged over something minor would have to wait until 2010 for our young cop. Even then, he was taught to avoid most of the words that Gibson utilized to taunt his ex-girlfriend.

Our cop did have some experience with nunchucks. He understood the danger they can present. He borrowed a set of nunchucks from a friend during a phase of life that all young men go through. We refer to that phase of life as, "How many times can you be struck in the nether regions without changing your voice enough to qualify for an Austrian boys' choir?"

I don't want to make light of the incident. We stand firm, believing it to be out of bounds for anyone who would be interested in being a future spokesman for motorcycle safety.

The lady went home. She was shaken, and stirred, by what she had experienced.

Our cop stayed in the area for a time, hoping that the psycho cyclist might come out of hiding so that we could chat with him about the importance of keeping both hands on the handlebars.

Paninis and Vice Presidents

I once avoided using a story about a man who had been sleeping at the Hannibal Hamlin Park in downtown Bangor.

 He had been moved along several times and, the last time he was spoken to, he had to remove a small tent that had been pitched near the former United States Vice President's statue.

I felt that since he seemed to have picked up on the message, it was old news.

The next week, he moved back in. He made himself more comfortable by pitching a much larger tent and plugging a toaster oven into the outlets that were installed to be used in illuminating festive downtown Christmas lights.

I will be upfront with you. I love it when someone who lives off the land finds a way to make their crib more comfortable. However, there is an ordinance against most of what the man was doing, and we had to move him along.

Since there was no refrigerator handy, the man's Natty Daddies needed to be consumed quickly and frequently. Room temperature—or in this case, tent-temperature—malt liquor makes urban camping much less glamorous. Drunk men in a tent, near a statue of a statesman, do not make other folks overly comfortable during the taking of historical selfies and quiet walks through the picturesque park.

The man was charged with drinking in public and criminal trespass since he had been warned for both of the crimes several times in the recent past. A house guest of the suspect was also asked to move along but was allowed to finish toasting his panini before the oven was disconnected from the city-supplied power.

There isn't a police officer in the city who is not going to allow you to finish melting the cheese on your panini. We are not Neanderthals. We might not be from Wisconsin, but we know the value of cheese in its heated and semi-solid state.

TC's Maxim #897: A panini prepared by pirated power probably plies the palate properly even after the po-po pulls the plug.

Performing in Porn
Over on Patton Street

Cops were called to a top-floor apartment on the east side of the city.

The report was that the tenants in this particular dwelling were yelling, arguing, and "stomping around" in a manner that bothered the others who sheltered just below them.

Upon knocking on the door, the cops met a male and a female who will remain nameless in this particular missive.

The man said that they were arguing but that any thumping happened when he tried to exit the room and found himself tripping over a fairly enormous dog.

The pooch appeared none the worse for the wear, and he stared at the officer in a way that indicated he might appreciate a bit of peace and quiet from his roommates. He then meandered off to a corner and only participated further in the gathering by sleepily observing and not committing his opinions to the discussion.

One of the officers could tell that even the dog was frustrated with the proceedings. The thing is, the two people who adopted him—during a fairly mundane celebration of unity and love at a local shelter—could be very annoying. The good news was that the dog never wanted for a funny story to re-gurgitate to the other dogs in the neighborhood.

The man then told the officer that his lady friend had recently confronted him with the theory that he was performing in some locally produced pornographic films. The fight had much to do about him doing nothing at all, at least, according to him.

While the officer wanted to ask more questions, he suppressed his immediate concerns for fear that he might say something inappropriate, even if by mistake.

We all have questions, but some of those questions should never be allowed to roll off the tongue.

The officer turned his attention to the lady of the house. She said that, while they did argue, there had been no inappropriate contact or an assault of any kind.

There was nothing left to do but warn the couple about the volume of their message. The cop told them to turn the volume back a notch, watch out for the dog—who was now safely on the couch—and to call if they needed any support in the form of law enforcement aid or intervention.

If this event had been a movie, the dog would have been the star; at least, he was a star in our eyes. We moved on and are being careful what we watch on late-night cable TV; no one needs to be surprised by what we saw there.

Peter, William, and Jerry

Two cops went to a Broadway address in order to speak to a man who had been reported to us as "being disorderly."

Upon their arrival, they met with Peter, William, and Jerry. The trio was a little upset, but it was not because every time they stated their names in front of folks who grew up in the late '60s—who were more than likely suffering from some minor hearing loss—would expect them to break into a rendition of "Puff the Magic Dragon."

These guys literally all had hammers and utilized those same hammers all over this land. The thing was, they were tradesmen who were trying to replace the vinyl siding on a building at that location.

They complained to the cops that a tenant of the building (who had been drinking whiskey from a jar) was throwing things at them as they went about their business. In a more country-musical way, drinking whiskey from a jar is certainly an accepted practice. It's just not as cool if it's dirty, or formerly held pimento-stuffed olives.

These guys were not even whistling anymore because the intoxicated tenant was being such a buffoon.

Our astute young officers found that the suspect, standing in front of the third-floor window, had already launched a window fan, a window blind, and an onion at the non-singing trio.

We all know that a cleanly peeled onion can make one cry, especially if you are struck by the root vegetable after it is hurled toward you at a high velocity from a third-floor window by a buffoon who is drinking whiskey from a dirty olive jar.

Let's not blame the onion, though. There are laws preventing the use of any root vegetable in a criminal act.

Although we will admit that if the man had thrown a carrot—or even a rutabaga—I would have had more fun writing today's story, but someone could have lost an eye in the meantime. Peter had already been struck by a window shade.

While being struck by the shade didn't hurt him badly, he determined that the man might move on to using small appliances in future attacks. Escalation is a common theme among those who consume their whiskey from a jar.

Peter shared his story while using calm tones and utilizing his peaceful personality. He represented the original trio quite well.

Peter never mentioned he would write a song about it—but even if he did—we felt the lyrics would not have been belted out in a harmonious manner, especially since he was the only member of this trio who was actually named after a member of the original group.

Additionally, Jerry's singing voice sounded far less like Mary Travers and much more like Tiny Tim. Did I mention he did have a hammer? Probably.

The third-floor window opened again, and our officer looked directly at the whiskey-soaked slinger of all that is available and advised him to stop throwing vegetables and, of course, other window parts.

Immediately, the man threw a random window screen at our cop. The officer stomped up the stairs to meet the gentleman on a more level playing field. Being the subject of random objects raining from above is not a pleasant place to be, even for the police.

Once our flat-foot met with the man, it was made clear that the times, they are a-changin'. He was told to stop, or he would be leaving, and not on a jet plane but in the back of a Ford Explorer with plastic seats and no snack service. We don't even have pretzels.

The suspect was found to be drunk, but that was a given.

Stomping back down the stairs with the satisfaction of a good warning given, our officer planned on leaving and letting the trio get back to creating a warmer and safer home for the inebriated man who was out of salad fixings and running low on whiskey.

That's when the Tide Pod came down from the heavens—and yes, we were surprised the gentleman did not eat it. He just seemed like the type.

Our answer was blowin' in the wind, as a slight breeze from the north took the VOVC (Vessel of Vibrant Colors) off its intended course, and it headed directly toward the melon of our lawman. The ACOCAFL (Airborne Capsule of Clean and Fresh Laundry) fell harmlessly to the ground nearby.

More stair-stomping followed, and the man was arrested for assault (for his original screen-play when the window shade struck Peter) and for disorderly conduct.

Peter, William, and Jerry were told that the day is done and that this land was now their land as we were removing the stewball to a more appropriate setting.

We are positive that the Penobscot County Jail makes sure all onions are chopped finely before they are served, and we are positive that the screens are not removable. He will be fine.

There's a short story for you. Go tell it on the mountain.

Potholes

A man who was riding around town on his motorcycle found that the plethora of potholes on some city streets made it difficult for him to enjoy himself.

While avoiding one riddled section, he hit a curb and crashed.

Our officer—who was nearby at the time—heard the crash and drove over to see what happened.

The man was uninjured, but he appeared to be under the influence of alcohol or drugs. Before he attempted to perform the officer's chosen field sobriety tests, the man produced three baggies of cocaine and told her that he would rather get this part of the stop out of the way, right off the bat.

He then admitted that he had been drinking.

We understand. The man was smashed, then crashed, broke spokes, and surrendered cokes (three bags-full, so we made it plural).

Could this day get any worse? Yes. Yes, it could. He was taken to jail as he was found to also be on probation for a previous DUI, so his probation officer put a long-term hold on him at the jail.

As with most things in life, we all whine loudly about the potholes, but they are usually the least of our worries.

Pull the Shade in the Key of D

We don't mind your calls. That's why we're here.

The truth of the matter is, we cannot fix every problem for every person. This was one of those cases.

A man on the east side called with a conundrum that was blatantly clear to him. It was clear to us, too.

His issue was with his neighbors. They lived across the street, and they had a habit of changing their clothing in front of their window.

I suppose, in order to be more clear, I should say that they stood in front of their own window during the phase that commonly occurs in between the donning and the doffing of daywear.

This is the period of time that is commonly considered— by most Americans—as being completely naked.

Our complainant—we will call him Dave—was dissatisfied with the day-in and day-out display of the duo's delicates.

Do tell, Dave. Do tell.

Dave couldn't be doubly sure if the man and woman ever wore clothing. One thing was downright certain, Dave was not dealing well with the daily display of their more devilish visual declarations.

Dave claimed—and I am paraphrasing here—that he was dumbfounded that the time period between the couple's state of dress—and undress—lacked all decency. Dave demanded that they draw the drapes, dim the LEDs, or at least duck down when drawing attention to their dynamite and dumplings.

Dave clearly wanted us to double dare the dipsticks to delete their lack of decorum. Dave longed for the drab days when daylight delivered a view of decent neighbors who were displaying a pair of dungarees, a dress, or even a double-breasted jacket, as dour as that might be deemed by those who dress more dapperly.

Our cop said, "Dang, Dave, we will give their doorbell a ding-dong and deliver—with discretion—your message of decorum before daylight savings time deletes the period of time where darkness gets a détente, and their daily decadence destroys any hope of decency."

The cop did what he told Dave he would do, but neither one of the undignified duo would come downstairs and discuss their obvious deference to ever needing even one delivery from the dry cleaner just down the street.

Darn it, Dave. We were diligent in our delusion that our delegation would draw out at least one of the defendants. In our defense, it's difficult to defuse those who deem it dignified to be de-clothed during all hours of the day or darkness.

Even our use of a dial-up device left us in a quiet depression.

In the end, Dave was dejected when our cop said, "The best offense is a good defense, buy your own drapes and draw them diligently."

Ramming Speed

The trouble with parking lots is that people go there, and then they park. We have documented exactly zero trouble in parking lots where there were no people, or cars.

We tend to believe that it is people who are the problem. Studies continue.

A police officer was asked to respond to an active verbal disagreement in the parking lot of a big box store that is well known for its value pricing. Pajamas are often the chosen uniform of some shoppers, and often those pajamas are not appropriate attire for sleeping, let alone shopping. I digress.

A man called to report that a woman in the lot was intentionally ramming her shopping cart (referred to in the south as a "buggy") into cars parked in the vicinity of her automobile. This is disheartening—but not surprising—to those of us who try to be responsible people, or parkers.

The cop showed up and was immediately waved down by a man who pointed to the lady in question. He claimed that when he confronted her about the issue at hand—or out of it—she threatened to spray him with a derivative of oleoresin capsicum.

Cops, and other humans of the world, know this to be commonly called pepper spray. It should be said that the man did call it pepper spray, but I chose to be more scientific in my presentation. There is no real reason to learn the scientific name, but you might want to do so for the sake of future conversations when you think it might behoove you to appear to be more scholarly. In those cases, you should avoid being seen in your pajamas—don't ask me how I know.

The man claimed that as he placed his wares into his car, he heard a surprising thud near his trunk lid. Knowing that he had not kidnapped anyone, he focused on other people in the lot. He looked up to see that the woman in question had lost control of her cart. The buggy gained significant momentum on the downhill grade toward where his car was parked—and subsequently thumped.

It's probably time that I mention that a good plumber would know that S&#t rolls downhill, and the same could be surmised for carts or buggies. The woman was not a plumber, but she was prepared for what came next.

The man, now a victim of minor damage to his wheels, walked over and attempted to take a photo of the woman's license plate while he inquired why she had let this happen. He told the cop that he wanted documentation that might aid in her identification if it came to that. The woman said it was an accident. The man didn't like the answer.

It was then that the lady flashed her oleoresin capsicum

in a manner that made the man rethink continuing on with the now-angry encounter.

If I hadn't required you to learn the scientific term of pepper spray, you might now be thinking the lady was flashing something else. You were armed with appropriate information. You're welcome.

The man walked back to his car, and the lady retrieved her cart. It was then that the cart escaped her grasp again. This time it rolled into another unoccupied motor vehicle, also downhill from her location.

Newton's First Law of Motion is clear about what was happening. But we are scientifically positive that Newton never expected a white Ford Fiesta to prove him one hundred percent correct.

Enough about science. The man was more enraged about watching this happen again, and he called the cops.

Our officer spoke to the woman and found that she did not intentionally become involved in proving Newton was right. He tried to allay the concerns of the man and took the report of damage to the Fiesta in order to locate the owner.

Two things come to mind: Don't always assume that people do dumb things on purpose. And don't waltz up on a woman who is wantonly wielding a can of whoop-ass while you're all wound up after watching her—wide-eyed—whack a pair of well-parked wheels.

It's far better to consider the fact that some peeps are

armed with proper cans of highly propellable pepper spray while parked and packing produce.

Kindness can create kinship, and pleasant words—presented properly—practically repel a police response.

Pepper spray isn't always a peacemaker, either. Practice patience.

Please.

Rapid Roy the Neighborhood Boy

The neighbor of a local "burnout enthusiast" told an officer that the Mustang driver's antics were becoming a little annoying.

It seemed the neighborhood "Rapid Roy" (shout out to Jim Croce) relished the rapid removal of rubber and relinquished the required restraint regularly reserved for those who seek requiescence.

The complainant remained complimentary to Rapid Roy and told the cop, "Don't get me wrong, it was a great burnout, but I don't want him doing it over here." This was a nice break for our officer. It is not often that the complainant in a case respectfully regales us with such due regard for the suspect's commitment to being an annoying tenant of the planet earth.

It's pleasant to see someone who is a bit angry take a step back, and then step forward to embrace the opportunity to compliment the person who makes them feel that way. This is the America that I remember.

The officer then went and spoke to the agent of all that

spent rubber and testosterone. The Mustang driver—in my mind—was doing what all Mustang drivers dream of doing: A street dance that is only accompanied by the shedding of Goodyear's finest blend of rubber and steel belts.

The gentleman, who probably smelled like gas and oil, admitted that he had been the culprit and promised that he would go forth and sin nor more. A warning was issued—after all, it was a great burnout!

We have had no more complaints. Sometimes a kind word and a nudge can change behavior.

I truly believe that.

Rubbing the Revolver

Radio transmissions that start with the words, "Speak to the shirtless male" are a staple snack in the call-to-call diet of the American police officer.

It was no surprise to our officers that they were being put to such a task. Of course, we like to have a few additional details in order to muster the proper response.

In this case, the man was sitting on his porch at a mobile home park—shirtless—drinking liquor and rubbing a revolver all over his body. He also pointed it in several different directions, and this was concerning to the neighbors.

When the officers arrived, the man had already secured the weapon inside his home. He admitted to conducting himself—exactly—as the neighbors had described it. He made sure to advise the cops that while the revolver was loaded, it had not been cocked into battery during his display of same.

The man had run into law enforcement officials in the past, and they had taken many of his weapons—mostly knives and machetes, battle axes, crossbows, and swords—previously, for safekeeping. His speargun and blowgun had also been taken.

The man told the officers that he meant no offense with his antics and was vehement in denying that he wanted to harm himself, or anyone else.

The man had recently moved to Bangor from a state far, far west of here. The man accepted his charges of reckless conduct with a firearm and agreed to go to a local medical facility for a voluntary conversation about the situation.

You see, being shirtless is not a crime. It is but one of many available indicators that your dinner conversations with the family will be starkly different than those had by the many who choose other occupations.

A Screaming Roll on the Macadam

A man who was running—outside—in the area of a local motel drew very little attention from passersby.

A short time into the running, the man began hollering loudly. No one could make out the words, but they watched anyway. The patience of the American onlooker never ceases to amaze us. Since the advent of cellular phones with cameras, people tend to stick around longer at the scene of other people in distress.

We wish we could tell you that they cared about their fellow man, or woman, but we would be lying. Most people are just trying to capture footage that will give them that fifteen minutes of fame that we all allegedly are looking for.

It's probably better that the man began to drop and roll around in the travel lane of the road; this forced the more compassionate among the onlookers to call the police to give the man a hand.

The caller said that the person rolling around in the street was wearing a blue sweatshirt and a red bandana. Our cops rushed to the scene and found that the man had gone back into his room. Upon our knocking on the door to his room the man indicated that he was fine now.

Clearly, whatever had happened to the gentleman was easily cleared up by a quick jog, a fit of screaming, and a quick roll on the macadam.

Supreme Commander of the Bad Driving Division

A man who suddenly began to shout out orders like a drill sergeant made all the patrons of a convenience store feel extremely nervous. He left the parking lot in a motor vehicle, right after selecting a couple of Slim Jims and something cold and refreshing from the cooler.

One of our officers stopped the vehicle shortly after the call came in. The clerk from the store wanted the man told that he was never to return. It was clear that no one in the store enjoyed the order to do jumping jacks while shopping for last-minute snacks and supplies.

The man in question advised our officer that he had been at the market while working in an undercover capacity for the "bad driving division" of the Department of Driving Enforcement. We do not know of this governmental entity, but we don't know everything. The officer pried deeper to find out more about the man's true identity.

The consumer of two Slim Jims went on to say that the

police officer had just completed the test and that he had passed with flying colors.

It was only then that the man surprised the officer with a previously unknown detail. The man claimed that he was our high commander and a superior officer who worked undercover for our very own police department.

There wasn't much left to discuss at that point. The high commander was given the bad news and advised that he should not return to the convenience store in question. Additionally, the man was given an official notice to drive the point home. He said he would comply with the order but that he would address it later during a meeting that—to date—has never been scheduled.

It was probably an oversight. We are still trying to access the database of the "bad driving division." We will await further word from the Supreme Commander.

The Desk Officer Hears It All

A lady who had been seeking the attention of others through the use of the World Wide Web found a man who claimed his name was Ronald.

Her claim was that he was, and I quote, "My sugar daddy."

The desk officer—tasked with taking complaints at the front counter—is believed to have raised at least one eyebrow, even while trying to remain stoic and helpful.

The term "sugar daddy"—coupled with the name Ronald—certainly didn't roll off the tongue with the sexy smoothness that a sugar daddy might be so inclined to seek. Ronald certainly is a strong and powerful-sounding name. However, we naturally question the job title in situations like those presented to us, as we hear and see things that should remain secret.

Sadly, the lady had complied with some requests from Ronald. She admitted to sending him photos of herself in various stages of undress. In return for these photos, Ronald was to send her financial consideration in the form of cash.

The checks did arrive as promised. In total, the checks tallied up to the tidy sum of two thousand dollars. That's no chump-change for the exchange. But—you guessed it—the paper instruments were well-played and were found to be drawn on false accounts. The bank contacted the woman after the fourth check was returned to them. The bank then asked for their money back.

She had copies of the checks. They were drawn on a Nevada bank, but the address on the check displayed a post office box number in New Mexico. Ronald's claim was that he was from Missouri. We know that's called the "Show Me State," and it appears that she did just that for Ronald.

It turned out that Ronald—as a daddy—would be more aptly referred to by the name of an infamous Jell-O dessert that was so very popular in the 1970s.

That would be . . . "sugarless."

The Good, the Bad, and the Weed Salesman

The proprietor of an emporium that provides smokable and edible herbal calming agents to those who seek relief from pain and—sometimes—reality called us with concerns.

The legal sale of mood-altering lettuce—not romaine—is not germane to the topic at hand, but it gives me pleasure to provide background details that allow me to utilize the word, "romaine."

The—certified—cannabis clerk said that he had some concerns about a man who had been out in the parking lot.

He said the man was making people in the area feel uncomfortable. He described the man as wearing a camouflaged vest, a green shirt, and that he was wearing knee pads. He said that the man was also toting a holstered pistol. He had not seen him make any threatening gestures with the handgun, but he asked us to check on him.

We arrived quickly.

We discovered that the man was a tradesman, a carpenter, if you will. His clothing description was accurate, but the man was carrying a hammer in his tool belt, not a pistol. Since he was on a cigarette break from the installation of flooring, he'd left his knee pads on while standing near his truck.

Since there was no one else in the parking lot, we could not find out if anyone else felt uncomfortable with his presence.

We say smoke 'em if you got 'em.

The Sons of Katie Elder?

A group of brothers over on the west side of town were reported to have been involved in drinking, fighting, and carrying on.

Usually, when there is drinking—and fighting—carrying on is fully expected to occur. Therefore, we, the cops of BPD do not hold carrying on against most individuals. Especially if they are a band of brothers who are involved in drinking and fighting.

We saw the classic John Wayne film, *The Sons of Katie Elder*, more than once. What struck me as most interesting about that movie is that Dennis Hopper seemed so short. This is merely an aside, but I want you to know what it's like to spend time in the vast cavern that I refer to as my brain. I apologize.

This drinking, fighting, and carrying on reached a level of annoyance that the neighbors couldn't stand. They called, and they wanted it all to stop.

When the cops arrived, they found the door ajar—it could have been broken—and just inside the doorway they observed what appeared to be a two-on-one pig pile; no offense meant to pigs.

Clearly, this wasn't Philadelphia.

While brotherly love can manifest itself in strange ways, this DF&CO (Drinking, Fighting & Carrying On) had culminated in a steaming pile of inebriated humanity holding down one of the participants. He appeared strong, and he acted it prior to being pummeled.

The story that was relayed to us by one BOOB (Brother, Out Of Breath) was that the man on the bottom had slapped one of his brothers across the face. The bottom dweller (of the pile) had then repeated his offense four more times before the other two brothers attempted to put an end to his nonsense.

That is precisely when this pig pile—predicted many times by their parents—proceeded to become palinoia. The po-po participated in pulling the pile apart, partly out of pity, partly out of purpose to mitigate the possible permeating and excessive pain for the sibling pinned to the Pergo.

Once the mayhem became more manageable, the brother on the bottom concluded that he had caused his own headaches and admitted that he was on probation for similar behavior with OPP (Other People and Participants). His probation officer advised the cops that the man was not allowed the use of strong drink. Family time—of course—was acceptable.

He was advised that he was due for a bit more downtime,

but it would be at the local jail. He complied with their commands, but we believe it was only because he was a bit tired.

No further problems were reported regarding the—now smaller—band of brothers who were left behind to finish out the spirited game of Parcheesi. Yes, Parcheesi.

The Sudden Stop

A man who was asked to leave a club designed for people to observe other people in various stages of undress said, "No."

For the sake of the missive, this location will be referred to as the CFNS (Center for Nudity Studies). Yeah, it's an educational thing, but the man had gone "hands on" with some of the educators and that is not tolerated. It was time for him to move along.

During his exit, he broke the door in what can only be described as an intentional act. He then gave his own lesson in nudity. He screamed at other patrons, dropped his pants, and presented his buttocks to those in the parking lot. No one offered to add cash to his G-string, since he was traveling "commando."

When the officer arrived, the man broke into a run. The officer gave chase. More than likely the officer decided to place the man under arrest for criminal charges.

A benefit of the chase was that the officer hoped to be able to observe how the man would physically manage to "repackage his biscuits" while on a dead run.

The chase did not reach the cool factor of the foot chase in the movie *Point Break* because the man attempted to jump over a four-foot railing near the Margaret Chase Smith Federal Building.

The unfortunate result of that leap was that there was a four-foot drop just beyond the rail. The rail was intentionally placed there to protect folks from falling into a concrete parking area.

Doing the math, which is not my strong suit and probably one of the many reasons I became a police officer, the four-foot vertical jump followed by the subsequent four-foot fall works out to at least eight feet of vertical drop.

This is what allowed the officer (not our fastest runner) to capture the man soon after the chase began. The officer did not observe the rapid descent, but he did hear it. I should say he heard the man stop suddenly.

As they say, it is the sudden stops that hurt the most. The man was dazed but uninjured by the remarkable leap of faith.

He was arrested for Disorderly Conduct and Refusal to Submit to Arrest. He was given a criminal trespass notice not to return to the CFNS. He was then delivered, with pants on, to the most accommodating jail guards this side of the Kenduskeag Stream. Pants are mandatory at the Penobscot County Jail.

This Is a Quiz

Let's see if you would handle the situation any differently than our featured MOTW (Moron of the Week).

You have rented a hotel room. You enter that room and stay for about an hour. During your stay in the room, you take a shower, and you use two bath towels. After a refreshing shower, you have a quick nap under the nicely fitted sheets.

It is only then that you determine to go speak to the desk clerk and ask for your money back because the room does not offer the "luxury" that you were seeking. The desk clerk offers to return all but five dollars of your money because they will have to makeover the room. She explains that she can only give you that amount because it is clear that you have used the shower and the bed.

You become enraged, and you demand a refund of all your money. Law enforcement officials arrive after being notified of loud yelling in the lobby. Police then warn you that you must leave immediately, or you could be arrested for charges of criminal trespass. You determine that it is best to cut your losses and drive away in your car.

A short time later, you return while the cop is still taking statements from the desk clerk. You then confront the cop and demand that you get a written receipt for the original rental. It seems you have lost your copy.

Question: Should you have removed the 9.5 grams of cocaine from your pocket before you returned and were placed under arrest for the crime of criminal trespass?

Answer: Yes, you should have removed the cocaine. They do not accept cocaine as personal property at the county jail, and it is subject to seizure and bonus criminal charges.

I suspect that most of you would have passed the test, but not everyone studies as hard as you.

Tinder Love

A woman who wanted to make a complaint about a recent love interest made it clear that the short-lived relationship had taken a turn for the worse.

She told the cops that she only knew the man by a nickname and that she had met him during a quick search for long-term love on a phone application known as Tinder.

She did not hold back on the details, though we wish that she had never kissed and told us about it.

Still, there appeared to be a crime afoot, and we try to focus on problems found in the statutes that are supplied by Maine lawmakers, not lovemakers.

Initially, she was convinced that he was engaged in philogyny, but soon found out that he was more interested in using her apartment as a place of business; she explained that she recently learned he was a purveyor of narcotics. This is always disheartening.

Suddenly finding out the truth about a love interest after spending over three days learning all you need to know in order to take the relationship to the next level is a real shock to the hopeless romantic.

She said she did not want to get the man into trouble in regard to his successful business, but she shared that he was now using her charge card as a low-interest line of credit to run his enterprise. She said she had let him use her driver's license to enable him to rent a motor vehicle that he needed to make on-time deliveries to those who purchased his products.

It's tough to compete in today's drug world without a strategy and good logistics. Even she understood that.

She couldn't believe that, after their time together, he would betray her like this. We simply agreed that not everyone should be trusted, even when you believe you know someone well. There are some quality television programs where the married couple only meet after agreeing to become engaged. Three days is a long-term engagement.

Since she had told him she was going to make a report to the police about using her credit card, he told her that he was going to sell her social security number to someone in the city who needed it. She assured us that there was no way that he would do that.

Love is blind.

We merely provide this information as a warning to others who think they have found the love of their lives. Our suggestion is to spend at least four days together before you settle down. It's best to fully know someone before sharing your credit cards and social security information.

Heck, we are certainly no Doctor Phil, but it might even be prudent to hang out for a couple of weeks before committing to a lifetime of love and narcotics trafficking as a family.

Tool-Toting Shirtless Man

Our cop responded to a complaint of suspicious behavior down on Central Street. To be more specific, the call was about a shirtless male walking about and wielding a knife.

Momma always said, "Wear a shirt in public," but she never really specified whether or not it was rude to keep your knife unsheathed whilst window shopping in the downtown district.

Some lessons are assumed—or at least we believed that they were.

During the search—which was more of a quick gander—for a shirtless male wielding a knife, our officer was approached by a pleasant lady who was not carrying a knife. She must have received the memo about the benefits of wearing a shirt in public; she was smartly dressed. She claimed she had just seen a shirtless male wielding a knife over near Gomez Park.

When our officer arrived at the intersection of streets that allowed access to that park, he observed a man carrying a large hammer.

A cop sometimes needs to make an assumption or two. Certainly, no one phoned us about a man carrying a hammer. But the utilization of tools, kept readily at hand, is a trait that is sometimes connected, at least in some way, to men who are not wearing shirts.

Now, the action of estimating or concluding something by assuming that existing trends will continue, or that a current method will remain applicable, does ring true in the fertile mind of a cop. It is sometimes referred to as "extrapolation."

Our cop extrapolated at an astounding rate and made the decision to confront the man with the hammer, even if it was only to inquire if he might have seen a shirtless man carrying a knife. I should also clarify that even though this hammer-wielder was wearing a shirt, he seemed a bit unkempt. Sometimes, a long stint of primping or tucking is completely uncalled for.

The chances of running into two different men, one of them shirtless, on a seventy-five-degree day are quite high in Maine. However, finding both men carrying tools that should normally be kept sheathed or boxed—possibly bagged, in the case of the hammer—certainly shaves off at least a percentage or two in the chance department.

When the cop inquired about the dissimilar similarities, he noted that the man was carrying both a knife *and* a hammer in the same hand. What are the chances? We say slim, even though the man was not.

Yes, we know that without wearing a shirt, there are limited locations to secret away both sharp and dull objects, but pants have pockets, and they should be used when roaming around in public areas with tools normally reserved for cutting and pounding.

I kid you not when I share that the man's explanation went as follows:

Cop: "Were you walking over on Central Street flashing that knife around while shirtless?"

Man: "No, but I was running shirtless."—This is what cops refer to as a "clue."

The man went on to explain that there was no real reason for him to be doing any of the aforementioned activities. The good news was that he had not threatened anyone. Other than alarming folks with his lack of attire and strange selection of both sharp and dull accouterments, his intentions were far from nefarious.

He gave the cop his hammer and his knife for safekeeping and promised to avoid similar activity for the foreseeable future. He was somewhat confused and agitated that someone had called the police to look into something so innocent.

The cop considered speaking to him about the fact that his mother probably had warned him of the dangers of running with sharp objects, but since he was now walking responsibly, the cop felt that he would be merely nagging.

These times do try us.

Very Vulgar Fare

A woman—described as loud and "very vulgar"—refused to exit the cab she had used to convey her drunken soul back to her abode. The cab driver was frustrated and concerned as the woman had become silent.

The transition from vulgar to silent is concerning if it happens immediately without warning.

Cab drivers are underpaid, over-informed, and underappreciated. They hear it all. They have to play along in order to make sure they are compensated for the headaches that are provided—gratis—from the riders that believe that they have something interesting to say. Many late-night travelers use the service because they are too drunk to drive.

If you are too drunk to drive your car, do you think you are sober enough to have a meaningful conversation?

Keep this in mind when you are liquored up and travel by cab. Also, make sure you tip your driver.

This cabbie did the right thing and called upon Bangor's Finest to check on the woman and get her out of his cab. Of course, his concern was driven by his desire to get paid and get back out on the town in order to transport other similarly impaired individuals back to their respective resting pods.

The officer—using skills honed in the downtown region—determined that the woman was asleep.

With the vocal tones that some have compared to a chain in a blender, as well as Connie Francis in her prime, he was able to coax the silent and somnolent specimen into some semblance of a supraliminal state of mind. Suddenly, she slipped out of her soporific state.

In other words, the cop woke her up without getting punched in the face.

She exited the cab and walked right into her home. The easy rider had become the easy strider, and she had not paid the fare.

The cabbie decided to cut his losses, as he did not want to return to collect, nor did he ever want to hear voluminous vulgarity from the vehement vixen of verboten free-loadin'.

Walking Tall—Louisville Edition

A woman reported that her neighbor—a lady—was outside working the woman's car over with a baseball bat.

We went quickly; we have seen *Walking Tall.*

When our officer arrived, he could clearly see that the car had been given the full and deluxe taillight customization service—including complete destruction—a smoothing of the upper doors for a more sporty and sleek appearance, and that included the violent removal of the side-view mirrors. The package is commonly referred to as the Buford T. Pusser Memorial Inside and Outside Car Detailing Service.

The complainant advised the officer that when she went outside to tell the customizer that she had not ordered this package, she was confronted with angry words from the impromptu detailer. Her credit card was not requested. It's apparent that this package is sometimes given free of charge.

Word was that the bat-wielding body customizer told the woman that she should stop spending so much time with the spouses of other individuals. Well, I'm paraphrasing, but you get the idea.

An innocent but helpful bystander advised he had watched the best show on the side street, and that he saw where the customizer had gone to hide. He led the cop to a door at an adjacent apartment house. He then left quickly. There are smart people out there. We had run into just one of them.

Our officer noted that there was a Louisville Slugger (32 oz.) leaning against the wall. His dad had always told him that if he was going to do a job, he should have the best tools available. He knew he was about to meet a craftswoman of the first order.

He knocked. A lady answered. The officer inquired if she had been out smacking cars and she said she had been inside her apartment for over four hours. He asked if she had a baseball bat. She told him that she did not have a bat. Simple and congenial conversations led the woman to tell the cop that her boyfriend might have been spending too much time at the driveway—and apartment—in question.

In the meantime, another witness came forward and told the backup officer that the woman they were speaking to had just returned to her apartment right after destroying the neighbor's car. He pointed toward the bat and recognized it as the tool that had been utilized to completely update the appearance of the automobile.

Our officer Colombo'd the woman with the following statement, "We are going to take that bat off the steps." She said, "You are taking my bat?" He said, "I thought you said it wasn't your bat!" She said, "You're right! I don't have a bat!" Further conversation led the woman to advise them that there was a minor chance that her DNA might be on the bat, but that it might not be.

She was charged with criminal mischief and banished from being involved in any more car customization and detailing for the foreseeable future.

She is no longer practicing her craft. After all, we did take her tool kit.

We Are the FBI, Just Google Us

The art of pulling off the ultimate scam has been sidelined by the fact that phone and internet miscreants have deduced that you can be just as successful by going for sheer volume rather than wasting your time with a cleverly devised and implemented plan.

Cops see it in our job, weekly. While the world loves to collectively agree that they would never fall for such idiocy, they do. It happens all over America. Every. Single. Day. This is just one story.

Our officers were sent to a home on the east side of Bangor where a woman who could be considered young—by all world standards—had just fallen victim to yet another phone-centric scam artist.

I merely share that she was young because sometimes the overwhelming public sentiment leads us to believe that only the older citizens are falling for this trickery and deceit. That's just not true. We believe that those who are above retirement age might be more likely to pick up the phone, but younger, well-educated Americans also fall victim to scams.

It seems that the woman had received a phone call from a man claiming to be from the Federal Bureau of Investigation. He told her that an abandoned and burned-out motor vehicle had been discovered somewhere deep within Mexico. His condescending manner relayed to her that documents—bearing her name—had been found inside the car. These "documents" proved that she had been engaged in laundering millions of dollars in dirty drug money. She was aghast at the thought.

Burned-out cars below the Rio Grande don't tend to extinguish themselves before most of the documents in the car are reduced to ash. That's something to consider if you receive a similar phone call.

Something else that she didn't think about was the fact that she was not involved in a world-wide money-laundering syndicate. She was not involved in any criminal drug trade. She had never been to Mexico, and she could easily pass a background check for almost any job in America. This is something we refer to as a clue in our industry.

Now, keep in mind that the words of the scammer made it clear that all of this criminal conduct could be cleared up with her generous purchase of some Home Depot gift cards.

She told him that she didn't believe what he was telling her—good on her. The man told her that if she didn't believe that he was in the FBI, she should use Google to look up the number that he was calling from. He advised that she should see that his exact phone number came back listed to none other than the Federal Bureau of Investigation.

She did. She found that the number was in fact listed as belonging to the FBI.

We should take a break in the action. All of you need to know that a caller's phone number can easily be masked and be shown as coming from another location or phone number. The lady did not know this. Once she used Google, she became terrified about being implicated in such heinous criminal activity.

The man, who was not from the FBI, then told her that unless she verbally delivered to him the tracking numbers located on the back of many, many Home Depot gift cards (all gift cards have a number that can be used to collect the balance) he would not be able to hold off the local law enforcement. He said he would send the cops to her house, and she would be arrested and delivered to federal authorities.

The poor woman then went to the local big-box store of all that is wood and shingles and spent over five thousand dollars. This was her entire life savings.

She later gave the man the numbers in a follow-up phone call. It was over four hours later when she notified our department of what she had done. While none of this is humorous or even induces a weak smile, I felt it prudent to include.

No federal agency or purported authority will ever ask you for gift cards of any kind. They cannot reduce the number of your alleged outstanding warrants in exchange for your credit card information. When in doubt, call your local police department.

Talk to your loved ones, let them know that they are to call *you* when they receive a call from someone who asks them for money in exchange for anything, including their freedom. Better yet, hang up on anyone asking for anything. Don't let your generous spirit be tainted by worry about making a person unhappy when you click your phone in their ear.

Encourage friends and loved ones to contact their own police department by using the number that can be obtained from that police department's website. Have them ask a close friend to go with them to the local police department so they can speak directly to the police officers there.

Remember, calling back the phone number that a person has utilized to mask their actual phone number will not lead to a conversation with the scammer. Calling that number will lead you to the proper agency. Inquire whether the name of the scammer is familiar. It won't be.

When Just Enough Is Too Much

A man who was reported to have been shoplifting at the local grocer was able to get one-hundred-and-ninety-three-dollars' worth of products into one medium size shopping bag. He was snagged at the front door before he could appreciate the sweet smell of freedom.

He did threaten to punch the clerk but determined that it was better to avoid an assault charge. Besides, his arm was tired from carrying the extremely heavy bag of secreted sweets and soda.

Once all the items were tallied, the manager indicated to our officer that the reusable cloth shopping bag—valued at five dollars—had also been stolen prior to the man filling it up. He wanted it added onto the amount that would need to be paid back in restitution if the man were ever to be convicted during a future court date.

The shoplifter was incensed by the manager's assertion that the bag was being added to the total. At that time the manager upped the ante by informing the man that the eight-pack of Diet Pepsi in the pile of booty came with a state mandated bottle deposit of five-cents per bottle. This made the shoplifter even more angry as he surmised that since the bottles had not been sold, he should not be responsible for the theft of the forty cents.

We get it. Make your best attempt, then run. But every man has a line that he won't cross, and in this case, it was paying for a bottle deposit.

The cop raised one eyebrow and then the other. He found himself agreeing with the power shopper and felt that adding the deposit on to the future restitution might be adding insult to injury.

While the manager was not happy about it, he understood the dilemma.

All three men—brought together with an apparent perfect alignment of one man selling, one man stealing, and one man serving a summons—eyed the unopened bag of Chips Ahoy Chunky Chocolate Chip Cookies and knew that in a different time and place they could have been friends with chocolatey smiles on their stern little faces.

We urge everyone to pay for their groceries—and bring your own bags.

Woman on a Bike

A woman who was riding a bicycle near the intersection of Union Street and Griffin Road took a nasty fall.

A cop who was sitting nearby helped her to her feet. She thanked him for his service to the community. She then tried to pedal off quickly.

Gathering up her name for the paperwork led the officer to discovered that, not only did she possess a bad sense of balance, but she also had multiple outstanding arrest warrants for failure to appear in court.

She was taken to jail, but not before we delivered her bicycle back to her driveway. We are hopeful that she has better balance in the future.

Falling down is just the first step in getting up again.

You Still Owe Me Fifty Bucks

A woman called our agency to report that she was in the company of a man who still owed her fifty dollars for a loan that she bequeathed him a few weeks before.

She said he was currently sitting in her kitchen and wondered if we could stop over and mediate the issue.

The officer stopped by—fully knowing that he could not make the man pay her back because it was clearly a civil issue between consenting adults. While he spoke to the duo, the woman said she knew that the man also had two outstanding arrest warrants.

The man who had refused to pay his debt looked at her with immediate disdain. He said that she'd promised not to say anything. This, in turn, brought about a conversation pertaining to promises made and promises broken.

With no other choice in the matter, our officer took the man to the county jail for the outstanding warrants.

The woman—who did have a smug look on her face—probably won't get her fifty bucks anytime soon. We will also say that it appeared to our officer that she didn't care any-more.

The moral of the story is that you should pay your debts to both your friends and society.

Levity—An Afterword

Levity has its place in this job. It has been a common thread for me and my connection to fellow police officers. We have laughed at inappropriate things and at inappropriate times. If you have been involved in public safety in any way, shape, or form, you have done the same thing. You know why it happens, and you know why it helps.

The humorous things that we see and share never outweigh our resolve to make sure that we do our best for our citizens and our community. We will always strive for perfection, but we will never, ever, be able to attain it. We are human, just like you.

We have flaws, we screw up, we go too slowly, we go too fast, we speak too much, and we speak too little. We say the wrong things, hoping that it will come out right. Sometimes we say the right thing at exactly the right time, and we are proud of ourselves.

I can tell you this: I have been proud to do this job for a very long time, and I am elated and proud to do it with such a fine group of police officers as those that I have worked with each day. Not one of them is perfect. We do not hire saints or angels as they never seem to fill out applications.